The Treacherous World of the 16th Century
&
How the Pilgrims Escaped It

The Prequel to America's Freedom

William J. Federer

Cover design by Dustin Myers LongitudeDesign.com

Picture credits: *Mayflower II on the Open Seas* by Montague Dawson (1890-1973); *The Departure Of The Pilgrim Fathers* by Bernard Finegan Gribble (1872-1962).

Library of Congress
WORLD HISTORY / UNITED STATES HISTORY
ISBN-13: 978-0-9896491-4-8

ebook
For a limited time, you may receive a digital copy by emailing **wjfederer@gmail.com,** with the subject line **"Pilgrims"** and a pdf file will be sent by reply email.

Amerisearch, Inc.
1-888-USA-WORD, 314-502-8924
wjfederer@gmail.com
www.AmericanMinute.com

*I always consider
the settlement of America with
reverence and wonder,
as the opening of a grand scene
and design in Providence
for ... the emancipation of the
slavish part of mankind
all over the earth.*

-John Adams,
*Dissertation on Canon &
Feudal Law,* 1765

America ... appears like a last effort of divine Providence in behalf of the human race.

-Ralph Waldo Emerson,
The Atlantic, April Issue, 1862

CONTENTS

All liberty is individual liberty.

-Calvin Coolidge,
Address to the Holy Name Society,
Washington, D.C., September 21, 1924

1. INTRODUCTION

Why are the Pilgrims so significant?

To answer that, one must understand the world in which they lived — a world ruled by kings.

How exceptional was it for this small group of Christians separatists in the early 1600s to attempt to rule themselves?

The fledgling American colonies were birthed out of vastly different circumstances. Their intertwining experiments of self-government wove together to birth a country unprecedented in equality and individual liberty. "All liberty is individual liberty," explained President Calvin Coolidge, September 21, 1924.

In order to fully appreciate the Pilgrim experiment, the stage has to be set. One must understand the dynamics at work in an era of global monarchs to see the truly profound paradigm shift which began in colonial America.

What were the emerging conflicts economically, politically and religiously, between Christians and Muslims, and between Catholics and Protestants, which turned Europe from facing east to facing west?

The main players in this drama were: the Ottoman Empire; the Spanish Empire; France; Holland; and England, with a supporting cast of Scotland, Sweden, Russia, Persia, and Italian city–states.

Much of this history reads like a soap opera, as the royal families of different countries were intertwined with marriage alliances.

America makes its entrance onto the world stage when the Ottoman Muslim Turks cut off land trade with India and China, giving impetus for Columbus to set sail looking for a sea route, but instead of the Far East, he ran into the New World.

Spain claimed most of the New World as their own for nearly a century, with the exception of a few Portuguese territories. Spain used gold and silver from Aztec and Inca Empires to finance its navy in stopping the Ottoman Muslims from taking over the Mediterranean and invading Europe.

In the midst of this, France did the unthinkable in making treaties with Spain's enemy – the Ottoman Empire. In addition to fighting the Ottoman Empire, Spain also fought the Protestant Reformation, sending its army and navy to invade Holland and England.

When Spain was repulsed, England and Holland grew to become global trading powers. They, together with other European countries, endeavored to settle colonies in the New World.

During Europe's religious wars, indefensible injustices were committed by and against all sides, Protestant, Catholic and Islamic. The purpose of reciting this history is not to rekindle ancient animosities but to understand the world from which the Pilgrims fled.

The Pilgrims intended to sail to the English colony of Jamestown, but, due to a storm, they landed in Massachusetts. There they began a tiny experiment of self-government.

This experiment flourished and spread into other New England colonies. After a century and a half, it laid the foundation for a nation governed by "the consent of the governed," and, as the Declaration of Independence acknowledged, that "all men are created equal … endowed by their CREATOR with certain unalienable rights."

Why is it so important to rediscover this history? Will & Ariel Durant wrote in *Lessons of History* (1968):

> Civilization is not inherited; it has to be
> learned and earned by each generation anew;

if the transmission should be interrupted ... civilization would die, and we should be savages again.

Roman orator Cicero stated in *Ad M. Brutum,* 46 BC:

Not to know what happened before you were born is to be a child forever.

Revisionists have employed a tactic called "deconstruction" – separating a people from their past, getting them into a neutral position where they do not remember where they came from, then brainwashing them into a planned totalitarian future.

It is like gene–therapy for a civilization, where the original DNA is removed so an altered, genetically engineered DNA can be inserted.

It is similar to a sales technique, namely: say negative things about the product a customer is currently using till they become repulsed by it. When they become open-minded to alternatives, you can give them a pitch for your new and improved product.

This technique is applied in education, where students are told negative things about their civilization's founders till they become repulsed by them. Then students become open–minded and malleable, allowing them to be easily persuaded to adopt alternative agendas.

Europe experienced this during the French Revolution, where they tore down statues, turned churches into "temples of reason," and even dug up graves of past leaders, like that of Good King Henry Navarre, and Ste. Genevieve, the patron saint of Paris.

The Soviets did this as well, changing the name of the city of St. Petersburg to Leningrad.

In 1933, Nazi leader Adolf Hitler burned books by Jewish authors, including Einstein. The poet Heinrich Heine prophetically penned in 1822: "Where they burn books, they will, in the end, burn human beings too."

Karl Marx stated:

> Take away the heritage of a people and they are easily destroyed.

Alexander Solzhenitsyn stated:

> If we don't know our own history, we will simply have to endure all the same mistakes, sacrifices, and absurdities all over again.

Harvard Professor George Santayana wrote in *Reason in Common Sense* (Vol. I, Life of Reason, 1905):

> Those who cannot remember the past are condemned to repeat it.

Ronald Reagan stated:

> Freedom is never more than one generation away from extinction. We didn't pass it to our children in the bloodstream.
>
> It must be fought for, protected, and handed on for them to do the same, or one day we will spend our sunset years telling our children and our children's children what it was once like in the United States where men were free.

Calvin Coolidge stated September 21, 1924:

> The principle of equality is recognized. It follows inevitably from belief in the brotherhood of man through the fatherhood of God. When once the right of the individual to liberty and equality is admitted, there is no escape from the conclusion that he alone is entitled to the rewards of his own industry ...
>
> It seems to me perfectly plain that the authority of law, the right to equality, liberty and property, under American institutions, have for their foundation reverence for God. If we could imagine that to be swept away, these institutions of our American government could not long survive.

Any hope of preserving America's freedoms is dependent upon citizens rediscovering the nation's profound origins, regaining a national identity, and appreciating how truly rare individual liberties are.

∾

2. HOW ISLAM LED TO THE DARK AGES

In just 12 years after Mohammed's death, 632–644 AD, the "rightly–guided" caliphs conquered the Eastern Roman Empire, Damascus, Syria, Jerusalem, Palestine, Mesopotamia, Eastern Anatolia, Armenia, Upper Egypt, Lower Egypt, North Africa, and most of Persia.

One of the most effective was Caliph Umar, who fought alongside of Mohammed in nearly all his 66 battles and raids. Umar's daughter, Hafsa, was one of Mohammed's wives.

Muslim pirates terrorized the Mediterranean and blockaded trade routes bringing economic disaster to Roman Europe by diminishing products moving from North Africa and the Middle East to Europe.

An important item no longer being shipped was papyrus, made from reeds along the Nile delta, which was used for paper in Europe. The sudden shortage of paper resulted in a decline of writing and literacy. This was a key factor in beginning what became known as THE DARK AGES, lasting till the 10th century.

The world's largest and oldest library was in Alexandria, Egypt, but it was destroyed by Arab Muslim warriors, similar to present-day reports of ISIS destroying 100,000 ancient books in the Central Library of Mosul, Iraq.

Historical accounts were given by: Persian traveler Abd-Al-Latif of Baghdad (1162–1231); Jamal Ad-din Al-Kufti (1169–1248); and Syrian prelate Bar Hebraeus (1226–1286), that when Caliph Omar was asked in 642 AD what to do with the books in Alexandria's library, he told his commander Amr bin al-Ass:

> Touching the books you mention, if what is written in them agrees with the Qur'an, they are not required; if it disagrees, they are not desired. Destroy them therefore.

The account stated that the books were burned to heat the city's bath-houses for six months. Other libraries in Babylon, Syria and Greece met similar fates. More recently, *Breitbart News* reported April 13, 2016:

> ISIS militants also raided the Central Library of Mosul to destroy all non-Islamic books. "These books promote infidelity and call for disobeying Allah," announced a militant to the residents. "So they will be burned."

In 711 AD, Muslim jihad crusaders crossed the Strait of Gibraltar and conquered all of Spain. Pope Gregory III put out a plea for help. Charles Martel was able to stop the Islamic advance just outside of Paris at the Battle of Tours in 732 AD, just 100 years after the death of Mohammed in 632 AD.

The Song of Roland, the oldest surviving major work of French literature, commemorates the Muslim ambush and annihilation of part of Charlemagne's army at the Battle of Roncevaux in 778 AD.

Muslim Caliph Al-Ma'mun of the Abbasid Dynasty ordered raiders to break into the Great Pyramid of Giza in 832 AD to loot the ancient treasures.

This began the plundering of the Pharaohs' tombs across Egypt. Within a few generations, the collective memory of ancient Egyptian history was eradicated. This was followed by later jihad destruction of:

> city of Ani in Armenia; city of Sarai Berke in southern Russia; Buddhist statues in Afghanistan; museum of ancient Assyrian Empire; grave of the Prophet Jonah in Nineveh (Mosul, Iraq); threat of Ayotollah Khomeini

to destroy Cyrus' ancient Persian Persepolis palace; rioters trashing Egyptian mummies; destruction of ancient Syrian and Chaldean churches dating from era of the Apostles.

An Islamic Hadith stated:

Abu'l-Hayyaj al-Asadi told that 'Ali (b. Abu Talib) said to him ... Do not leave an image without obliterating it, or a high grave without leveling it. This hadith has been reported by Habib with the same chain of transmitters and he said: Do not leave a picture without obliterating it. (Hadith Bk 4, No. 2115)

As the "rightly guided" Muslim Caliphs conquered North Africa and the Middle East, and raided coasts of Europe, Mediterranean trade was interrupted. Rome and Byzantium were economically devastated.

In 846 AD, just 46 years after Charlemagne was crowned Holy Roman Emperor in Rome's old St. Peter's basilica, 11,000 Muslim Saracen warriors sacked Rome, looted St. Peter's basilica and the Basilica of Saint Paul Outside the Walls. They also desecrated the graves of both St. Peter and St. Paul. As a result, Pope Leo IV began building the wall around the Vatican.

In 849 AD, Muslim Saracen raiders set sail from Sardinia with a fleet to invade Rome. Pope Leo rallied the cities of Amalfi, Gaeta and Naples to send ships to block the mouth of the Tiber River near Ostia. Muslim warriors attacked and the fighting was fierce. Suddenly, a violent storm arose, dividing the Christians fleet from the Muslim attackers in the Battle of Ostia.

Christian ships were able to make it back to port and weather the storm, but the Muslim ships were severely damaged and scattered. When the storm subsided, the remaining Muslim ships were easily captured.

During Islam's Golden Age, from the 10th to 12th

century, the Islamic world almost experienced the Renaissance instead of Europe.

One Muslim scholar was Al Farabi (872–951 AD), who studied Greek science and philosophy. Another was Avicenna (980–1037 AD), a prominent Persian Muslim scholar who wrote 450 works on philosophy, medicine, and math. Averroes (1126–1198) was a Muslim philosopher in Andalusia–Spain who wrote on physics, music, geography, medicine, and math.

These scholars attempted to moderate Islam, even suggesting Paradise may not be a place of sensual gratification.

Their efforts, though, were abruptly ended by Ghazali (1052–1111), who was considered the single most influential Muslim after Mohammed. Being a "mujaddid" or "renewer of the faith" in Baghdad, Ghazali condemned moderate philosophers, writing:

> One should restrain anyone who would immerse himself in these mathematical sciences ... for even though they do not pertain to the domain of religion, yet, since they are among the foundations of the philosophers' sciences, the student will be infected with the evil and corruption of the philosophers.

Al Farabi, Avicenna, and Averroes did not succeed in keeping the Islamic world open to philosophy and science. On the other hand, Thomas Aquinas did succeed in the Christian West, giving momentum to the universities springing up in Catholic cities of Paris, Naples, Bologna, Toulouse, and Oxford, thus preparing the West to experience the Renaissance.

❧

3. CRUSADES

Travelers returned from pilgrimages to the Holy Land with reports of Muslim persecutions and cruelties toward "dhimmi" Christians. "Mad Caliph" Al-Hakim bi-Amr Allah ordered the Church of the Holy Sepulchre in Jerusalem to be destroyed in 1009.

When Vikings became Christian, they were referred to as Norsemen or Normans. In 1057, Norman adventurer Robert Guiscard sailed into the Mediterranean. He took control of Calabria in the "toe of Italy," and drove the Muslims out of Sicily.

In 1071, Muslim crusaders delivered a major defeat to the Byzantine Christians at the Battle of Manzikert, taking control of all but the coastlands of Asia Minor (modern-day Turkey).

In desperation, the Byzantine Emperor Alexius I Comnenus humbled himself and sent ambassadors to the Council of Piacenza in 1095, appealing for help from his religious rival, the Roman Catholic Pope.

Since Spain successfully drove Muslim warriors from Toledo and Leon by 1085, Pope Urban II made an impassioned plea for Spain, and other Western leaders attending the Council of Clermont in 1095, to send help to the Byzantine Christians, whom Muslims:

> "... compel to extend their necks and then, attacking them with naked swords, attempt to cut through the neck with a single blow." (Robert the Monk, *Medieval Sourcebook,* Fordham University.)

The First Crusade began in 1097. In the next two centuries, there were a total of 9 major Crusades to return the Holy Land to its pre-Islamic inhabitants.

Thomas Aquinas wrote in *Summa contra Gentiles,* 1258 (translated by Anton C. Pegis, University of Notre Dame Press, 1975, Book 1, Chapter 6):

> Mohammed ... seduced the people by promises of carnal pleasure to which the concupiscence of the flesh goads us ... and he gave free reign to carnal pleasure. In all this, as is not unexpected, he was obeyed by carnal men.

As for proofs of the truth of his doctrine, he brought forward only such as could be grasped by the natural ability of anyone with a very modest wisdom. Indeed, the truths that he taught he mingled with many fables and doctrines of the greatest falsity.

He did not bring forth any signs produced in a supernatural way, which alone fittingly gives witness to divine inspiration ...

On the contrary, Mohammed said that he was sent in the power of his arms – which are signs not lacking even to robbers and tyrants ...

Aquinas concluded:

Those who believed in him were brutal men and desert wanderers, utterly ignorant of all divine teaching, through whose numbers Mohammed forced others to become his followers by the violence of his arms ...

He perverts almost all the testimonies of the Old and New Testaments by making them into fabrications of his own, as can be seen by anyone who examines his law.

It was, therefore, a shrewd decision on his part to forbid his followers to read the Old and New Testaments, lest these books convict him of falsity ... Those who place any faith in his words believe foolishly.

After the Crusades ended, the Muslim jihad conqueror Tamerlane killed 17 million people across central Asia in the 1300s, annihilating Christianity. He left pyramids of human skulls in Delhi, India.

᷍

4. EASTERN EUROPE

In the 1400s, famous Eastern European kings and nobles courageously resisted the Islamic invasion:

•Sigismund, King of Hungary fought the Ottoman Turks, 1387–1437, forming the Order of the

Dragon, or Order of St. George the Dragon–Slayer, with the dragon being the Muslim Ottoman Sultan;

- •Prince Fruzhin fought the Turks in Bulgaria, 1406–1444; King Wladyslaw III fought the Turks in Poland, 1434–1444;
- •John Hunyadi fought the Turks in Hungary, 1438–1456;
- •Vlad the Impaler fought the Turks in Romania and Wallachia, 1444–1446;
- •George Kastrioti "Skanderbeg" fought the Turks in Albania, Venice, and Naples, 1444–1479;
- •Stephen the Great, "Athleta Christi," fought the Turks in Moldavia, 1457–1504.

In 1453, Ottoman Muslims invaded further into Byzantium and sacked Constantinople. Graves were desecrated and the largest Christian Church in the world, the Hagia Sophia, was turned into a mosque.

✑

5. HOW ISLAM LED TO THE RENAISSANCE

Ottomans invaders into the Byzantine Empire destroyed churches, schools, museums, and the graves of Christian saints. Greeks hurriedly fled with their treasures, literature, architecture, art, and philosophy to Florence, Italy.

This flood of ancient culture into Western Europe sparked a re-discovery of Greek civilization called the Renaissance.

Jean-Jacques Rousseau (1712–1778), considered one of the Fathers of the French Revolution, owned a dog he named "Sultan." He stated in his *Discourse on the Arts and Sciences,* 1750 (translated by Ian Johnston):

> Europe had fallen back into the barbarity ... A revolution was necessary to bring men back to common sense, and it finally came

from a quarter where one would least expect it. It was the stupid Muslim, the eternal blight on learning, who brought about its rebirth among us.

The collapse of the throne of Constantine carried into Italy the debris of ancient Greece. France, in its turn, was enriched by these precious remnants. The sciences soon followed letters. To the art of writing was joined the art of thinking.

President Obama referred to this in a speech in Egypt, June 4, 2009: "It was Islam ... paving the way for Europe's Renaissance."

In retrospect, Muslim warriors helped bring about the "Dark Ages" when they conquered Egypt, North Africa and Spain in the 7th and 8th centuries, cutting off trade across the Mediterranean and holding back ships of papyrus.

Additionally, Muslim warriors helped bring about the "Renaissance" in the 14th and 15th centuries, when they invaded Greece, causing Greek scholars to flee to Italy.

In fact, the very concepts of "Europe" and "Christendom" took shape in response to the Islamic invasion. Previously, European kingdoms viewed themselves as independent entities.

This is similar to the way the 13 American colonies viewed themselves as independent entities, but agreed to work together against Britain's King George III, giving birth to the concept of the "united" states.

As the wealth of the Greek Byzantine Empire flowed into Florence, Italy, many were made rich, most notably the families of Medici and Borgia, who financed artists Michelangelo and Leonardo DaVinci, and astronomer Galileo Galilei.

Through marriages, the Medici family influenced the major banking, political and religious powers for centuries in Spain, Austria, France, Holland and Italian states. Four Popes were from the Medici family:

- Pope Leo X (term 1513–1521), born Giovanni de' Medici;
- Pope Clement VII (term 1523–1534), born Giulio di Giuliano de' Medici;
- Pope Pius IV (term 1559–1565), born Giovanni Angelo Medici; and
- Pope Leo XI (term April 1, 1605–April 27, 1605), born Alessandro Ottaviano de' Medici.

Niccolò Machiavelli dedicated his notorious book, *The Prince*, 1515, to Lorenzo de' Medici "The Magnificent," who as the wealthiest and most powerful political leader in Florence during the Renaissance.

The Prince was considered a synthesis of the corrupt tactics of Cesare Borgia, the illegitimate son of Pope Alexander VI (r.1492–1503). Cesare Borgia, and his sister, Lucrezia, were infamous for their lust for power, adulteries, illegitimate offspring, deceit, betrayals, intimidation, poisonings, assassinations, incest, and murders for political advancement. These actions were embodied in the phrase, "the ends justifies the means."

Corrupt politicians ever since have employed this maxim to justify using immoral tactics to achieve their "end," which they have convinced themselves is "good."

Condemning the corruption, materialism and sensualism in Florence was Dominican friar Girolamo Savonarola (1452–1498), whose preaching sparked a Christian revival. Political leaders had Savonarola arrested, tortured, excommunicated and executed.

Christian refugees continued to flee the Islamic invasion of Greece. Among them were scholars who brought to the ancient Greek Bible manuscripts and Greek New Testament scriptures to Europe.

Soon, western European scholars, like Desiderius Erasmus (1460-1527), who corresponded with Martin Luther, translated the Bible not just from Latin, but from Greek. Erasmus published the first Greek translation of the New Testament in 1516, *Novum Instrumentum omne*. The interest in the original New Testament language of Greek helped begin the Reformation.

∾

6. AGE OF DISCOVERY

In the previous centuries Muslim Arabs, Turks, Mughals and Afghani conquerors killed tens of millions of Syrian Christians, Chaldean Christian, Jews, Hindus, Buddhists, Sikhs and others in the Middle East, Central Asia, India, and the East.

In the West, during this time, Spanish soldiers proved to be the most effective defenders of "Christendom" from Islamic jihad crusaders.

The fall of Constantinople in 1453 ended the Europeans use of the land trade routes, such as the Silk Road, which extended from China across India to Europe. As a result, Europeans looked for a sea route, beginning the Age of Discovery.

In 1497, King Manuel I of Portugal sent explorer Vasco de Gama to find an eastern route to the Far East by sailing around South Africa. He arrived in Calicut, India, in 1498.

In 1497, King Henry VII of England sent Italian explorer John Cabot to find a western route to the Far East. Cabot explored the coast of Newfoundland and down the coast to Chesapeake Bay, being the first European to see North America since the Vikings five centuries years earlier.

A few years before Vasco de Gama and John Cabot, King Ferdinand and Queen Isabella ended the 700 year Muslim occupation of Spain, and sent Christopher

Columbus in 1492 to find a western sea route to India and China. Convinced he had reached India, Columbus named the people he met "Indians."

It is a revelation to Columbus' detractors to turn one chapter back in the book of history to discover it was Islam's conquering of eastern land routes to India and China that caused Columbus to seek a western sea route.

Additionally, by comparison, Columbus' treatment of native inhabitants of America was demonstrably more considerate than Vasco de Gama's treatment of native inhabitants of India.

After Columbus' voyage, Spain claimed all the New World as its own, though Portugal was successful in convincing Pope Alexander VI to grant it Brazil and some islands in the south Atlantic.

❧

7. LIST OF SPANISH MONARCHS

Spanish monarchs Ferdinand and Isabella had a daughter, Catherine, who married England's Henry VIII.

Another daughter, Joanna, married the Austrian Hapsburg Prince Philip the Handsome, making him the King of Spain and the Spanish Netherlands.

After Philip's death, Joanna was considered mental unstable and committed to a nunnery, resulting in her name "Joanna the Mad."

Philip and Joanna's son was Charles V of Spain.

At this point it would be helpful to see a list of Spanish monarchs during this era:

Of the House of Trastámara were:

•Ferdinand V & II and Isabella I, co-reigned 1475–1516.

•Joanna the Mad and Philip the Handsome, co-reigned 1504–1516.

Following them, of the House of Habsburg, were:

- •Charles I and V, reigned 1516–1556, also being the Holy Roman Emperor, before he finally abdicated.
- •Philip II, reigned 1556–1598, married briefly to England's Mary I "Bloody Mary."
- •Philip III, reigned 1598–1621.
- •Philip IV, reigned 1621–1665.
- •Charles II, reigned 1665–1700.

❧

8. EMPIRE ON WHICH THE SUN NEVER SET

After driving the Muslim Moors from Europe in 1492, Spain grew to be the most powerful empire in the world, ruling nearly 2 million square miles – an "empire on which the sun never sets."

King Charles V oversaw Spanish exploration and colonization of the New World, claiming an almost monopoly control since its discovery by Columbus.

In 1512, Juan Ponce de León explored Florida, reputedly in search of the Fountain of Youth. He had named it "La Florida" as he explored it during the season of Pascua Florida ("Flowery Easter").

In 1514, Pedro Salazar of Hispaniola explored the coast between North Carolina and Georgia.

In 1516, Diego Miruelo explored Tampa Bay area.

In 1517, Francisco Hernández de Cordova explored southwest Florida. This same year, Martin Luther began the Reformation in Europe.

In 1519, Alonso Álvarez de Pineda mapped the Gulf of Mexico coast.

In 1519, Hernán Cortés landed in Aztec Mexico, conquering it for Spain in 1521.

In 1519, Charles V sent the Portuguese explorer

Ferdinand Magellan on the first voyage to circumnavigate the world. Sailing for Spain, Magellan began his search for a route to the East Indies by traveling down the coast of South America.

Magellan's fleet reached Cape Virgenes and concluded that they had found a passage because the waters were brine and deep. Four ships went through the 373-mile long passage which Magellan called "Estrecho de Todos los Santos" or "Canal of All Saints," as the date was November 1st, "All Saints' Day." It came to be called the "Strait of Magellan."

On the other side of the strait, Magellan saw the sea very still and peaceful, so he gave it the Portuguese name "Mar Pacifico" meaning "Pacific Ocean."

A few years earlier, the first European to see the Pacific Ocean was Spanish explorer Vasco Núñez de Balboa who had crossed the Isthmus of Panama in 1513. He named it "Mar del Sur" meaning "southern sea."

Magellan sailed for weeks without sighting land. His food supplies dwindled and rotted, and men began to perish from scurvy, malnourishment, and dehydration. They sighted a small uninhabited island, restocked supplies, and set sail again on January 28, 1521.

They reached the Marianas, Guam, and then the Philippine Islands, which were later named for King Charles V's son, Philip II.

Magellan communicated with native tribes through his Malay interpreter, Enrique. They traded gifts with Rajah (King) Siaiu of Mazaua who guided them to the Island of Cebu. On the Island of Cebu, Magellan met Rajah Humabon, who had an ill grandson. Magellan (or one of his men) was able to cure or help this young boy, and in gratitude Chief Humabon and his queen Hara Amihan were baptized as Christians, along with 800 of followers.

Afterwards, Rajah Humabon and his ally Datu Zula entangled Magellan in a conflict with a neighboring chieftain, Datu Lapu-Lapu of the Island of Mactan. Magellan had wished to convert Datu Lapu-Lapu to Christianity, but the chieftain was dismissive.

On the morning of April 27, 1521, Datu Lapu-Lapu with around 1,500 of his troops confronted the Spaniards on the beach. Magellan was hit by a bamboo spear, surrounded and then killed. His crew escaped and continued to sail their ship, *Victoria*, back to Spain, arriving in September of 1522. The Philippine Islands went on to become the most Christian nation in Asia.

In 1521, Ponce de León attempted a settlement near Charlotte Harbor, Florida.

In 1521, Pedro de Quejo & Francisco Gordillo landed at Winyah Bay, South Carolina.

In 1524, Francisco Hernández de Córdoba conquered Nicaragua, accompanied by Hernando de Soto.

In 1525, Pedro de Quejo explored the coast from Amelia Island, Florida, to the Chesapeake Bay.

In 1526, Lucas Vázquez de Ayllón explored the eastern coast of America as far north as Delaware Bay, then, somewhere near Sapelo Sound, Georgia, he and 600 settlers attempted a settlement named San Miguel de Gualdape. The Dominican friars who accompanying them celebrated the first recorded Catholic Mass in what would later be the United States.

Unfortunately, that winter, two-thirds of the settlers died of disease, including Ayllón. One hundred African slaves rebelled and ran off to live with the native tribe of Guales, being the first non-natives settlers in North America.

In 1528, Pánfilo de Narváez and Cabeza de Vaca led an expedition of 400 settlers to establish a settlement in Florida. Battered in a hurricane, they were shipwrecked near St. Petersburg. Natives misled, betrayed, and ambushed them. One member of the expedition, Juan Ortiz, was captured and enslaved by the Tocobaga tribe, being rescued 12 years later by De Soto's expedition.

The surviving 80 members of the Narváez expedition returned to the Tampa Bay coast. They salvaged their wrecked vessel and fashioned it into two rafts, using deer skins for bellows to blow air into the fire, making it hot enough to forge metal nails.

They floated along the coast of the Gulf of Mexico from Florida to the mouth of the Mississippi River, where they were suddenly swept out hundreds of miles.

Narváez was never found, and Cabeza de Vaca, with two dozen others, were shipwrecked near present-day Galveston. They were enslaved by natives, and only 4 escaped: Cabeza de Vaca, Andrés Dorantes de Carranza, Alonso del Castillo Maldonado, and Esteban, who had been a Moroccan Berber slave.

They traveled through the areas of Texas, Arizona, New Mexico and the Mexican states of Tamaulipas, Nuevo León and Coahuila.

Cabeza de Vaca preached the Gospel and prayed Christian prayers for sick natives to be healed, with reports of miraculous recoveries. Gaining a reputation as a "faith healer," the Indians let him travel freely.

Cabeza de Vaca and his companions came down the coast of the Gulf of California to Sinaloa, then finally to Mexico City in 1536, eight years after the expedition began.

Cabeza de Vaca sailed back to Spain He returned to the New World in 1540, as governor of New Andalusia (Argentina), where he helped settle Buenas Aires.

Back in Europe, Sultan Suleiman's 120,000 troops were laying siege to Vienna, Austria in 1529.

In 1532, Francisco Pizarro conquered Peru's Inca Empire, being accompanied by Hernando de Soto.

In 1535, Cortés explored Baja California and the Sea of Cortés.

In 1539, Hernando de Soto landed in Tampa Bay. He rescued Juan Ortiz, who related rumors of gold in Apalachee. De Soto seized Indians as guides. He was the first European to cross Georgia, South Carolina, North Carolina, the Great Smoky Mountains, Tennessee, Alabama, Mississippi, Arkansas, Missouri, Kansas, and Oklahoma. He died in 1542 near the Mississippi.

In his travels, De Soto passed through a native village named "Tanasqui." Over a century later, British traders encountered a Cherokee town named "Tanasi." Andrew Jackson suggested this as the name for the State of "Tennessee."

In 1540, Spanish Francisco Vázquez de Coronado sought the Seven Cities of Gold, traveling from Mexico through Arizona, New Mexico, Texas, Oklahoma and Kansas, viewing the Grand Canyon and Colorado River.

In 1542, Juan Rodríguez Cabrillo sailed up the coast of California.

In 1559, Tristán de Luna y Arellano attempted to settle Pensacola Bay.

In 1561, Angel de Villafañe attempted to settle Santa Elena in Port Royal Sound, South Carolina.

In 1565, Pedro Menéndez de Avilés destroyed Jean Ribault's French settlement of Fort Caroline, near present-day Jacksonville, then went on to found St. Augustine, Florida, the oldest continuously occupied European city in the continental United States.

In 1566, Pedro Menéndez de Avilés arrived at Parris Island, South Carolina, where four years earlier Frenchman Jean Ribualt had failed in an attempt to found

Charlesfort. Menéndez built a new fort, San Salvador, then a few months later, Santa Elena and San Felipe.

After 21 years, these settlements were abandoned due to hostile tribes, disease, and the encroachment of the English, with Sir Francis Drake raiding Spanish settlements, and Sir Walter Raleigh's Roanoke Island Colony in nearby North Carolina.

In 1567, Juan Pardo retraced the paths of Desoto, exploring parts of North and South Carolina, eastern Tennessee. He attempted the first European settlement in North Carolina–Fort San Juan at Joara.

In 1592, Greek navigator Juan de Fuca sailed on a Spanish expedition to find the rumored, semi-mythical Strait of Anian connecting Asia with North America, first mentioned in the adventures of Marco Polo. Two centuries later this was discovered to be the Bering Strait.

Nevertheless, in Juan de Fuca's honor was named the sea boundary between Canada and the State of Washington–the Strait of Juan de Fuca.

In 1595, Pedro Fernandes de Quirós was pilot on the expedition of Álvaro de Mendaña de Neira to colonize the Solomon Islands. When Mendaña died, Quirós took command, arriving in the Philippines.

In 1605, Quirós, supported by King Philip III and Pope Clement VIII, led 3 ships with 160 men on an expedition which discovered Henderson Island, Ducie Island, the Buen Viaje Islands (present-day nation of Kiribati). They sighted Tahiti and the Tuamotu archipelago island, then reached New Hebrides (present-day Vanuatu).

In 1606, Quirós planted a large cross on land he named "Australia del Espiritu Santo"–Australian Land of the Holy Spirit–which became the name of the southern continent of Australia. He intended to establish a colony there named "Nova Jerusalem," stating:

I, Captain Pedro Fernandez de Quirós ...
hoist this emblem of the Holy Cross on which
His person was crucified and whereon He gave
His life for the ransom and remedy of all the
human race ...

On this Day of Pentecost, 14 May 1606 ... I
take possession of all this part of the South as
far as the pole in the name of Jesus ...

From now on, shall be called the Southern
Land of the Holy Ghost [La Terra Australia
del Espiritu Santo] ... to the end that to all the
natives, in all the said lands, the holy and sacred
evangel may be preached zealously and openly.

Charles V's Spanish Empire stretched across
Europe, the Netherlands, the Far East, the Caribbean
to North and South America. It truly was "the empire
on which the sun never sets."

❧

9. BARTOLOME' DE LAS CASAS

During the "Spanish Century" or "Spanish Golden
Age," conquistadors often raided native villages and
took captives into slavery. Though these conquistadors
were tragically motivated by greed, there were also
Spanish missionaries motivated by the gospel.

This is the story of Bartolome' de Las Casas, who
left Spain in 1502 for the West Indies. He became
a hacendado (owner) of an encomienda (plantation)
where he owned native American slaves. He even
participated in slave raids and military expeditions
against the native populations of Hispaniola and Cuba.

In 1511, Las Casas' life changed when he heard a
sermon by Dominican friar Antonio de Montesinos:

I am a voice crying in the wilderness ... the
voice of Christ in the desert of this island ...
You are all in mortal sin ... on account of the
cruelty and tyranny with which you use these

innocent people. Are these not men? Have they not rational souls? Must not you love them as you love yourselves?

Montesinos continued:

> Tell me by what right of justice do you hold these Indians in such a cruel and horrible servitude? ... Why do you keep them so oppressed and exhausted ... from the excessive labor you give them ... in order to extract and acquire gold every day.

Bartolome' de Las Casas was stung in his heart by Motesino's preaching and determined to follow Jesus. He became the first priest ordained in the New World.

Las Casas' preaching was similar to the much later Civil Rights leader Martin Luther King, Jr., who stated:

> "The church must be reminded that it is ... the conscience of the state ..." and "It must be the guide and the critic of the state ... If the church does not recapture its prophetic zeal, it will become an irrelevant social club without moral or spiritual authority."

In 1514, while preparing a Pentecost Sunday sermon, Las Casas read from the Book of Ecclesiasticus (Sirach 34:18-22), that if one offers as the sacrifice of an animal that they have obtained dishonestly, it is unacceptable, and it is as murder to deprive someone of his means of making a living.

Las Casas dedicated the rest of his life to ending the enslavement of native Americans. He became Bishop of Chiapas and was officially appointed "Protector of the Indians."

In 1515, two years before his contemporary Martin Luther started the Reformation, Las Casas and Montesinos went back to Spain where they met with King Ferdinand on Christmas Eve. The King agreed with their cause to end the enslavement of native

Americans, but he died within a month without acting.

Las Casas, being now 40-years-old, petitioned the new 16-year-old King Charles V to end the military conquest of the new world and use peaceful means to convert Indians. This was the same King Charles V who, in 1521, presided over the Diet of Worms and the proceedings against Martin Luther.

King Charles V was also busy defending Europe against jihadist Muslim Turkish warriors of Sultan Suleiman the Magnificent, who attacked Hungary in 1526 and Austria in 1529.

In 1520, Las Casas founded three Christian Indian towns in Venezuela, but nearby Spanish encomiendas (plantation) owners stirred up natives to destroy them.

In 1531, on Tepeyac Hill outside of the former Aztec capitol of Mexico City, word spread of the Indian Juan Diego and his vision of the "Virgin of Guadalupe" which resulted in an estimate 15 million Indians being baptized in the next 20 years. Many consider this the largest mass conversion in history.

In 1536, Las Casas criticized Franciscan friar Motolinia for being too quick to baptize the thousands of Indians before they were fully instructed in the faith.

Las Casas wrote a treatise, titled: "Concerning the Only Way of Drawing All Peoples to the True Religion." This resulted in Las Casas being hated by those who profited off of slavery.

Similar to modern-day pro-life versus pro-abortion, Las Casas debated Juan Ginés de Sepúlveda in 1550 at Valladolid, Spain. Sepúlveda argued that Indians were less than human and therefore it was justified to enslave them; whereas Las Casas argued that Indians were indeed fully human, created in the image of God, and therefore should not be enslaved.

This conflict demonstrated the tension between

two threads running through history: GREED and the GOSPEL. People motivated by the GOSPEL:

- -gave money, food, clothes & shelter to the poor;
- -dug wells in native villages;
- -opened orphanages;
- -founded hospitals;
- -staffed medical clinics;
- -inoculated children;
- -took in homeless;
- -visited those in prison;
- -provided disaster relief and emergency aid;
- -taught farming techniques;
- -provided literacy programs; and fought to abolish slavery.

Those motivated by GREED:

- -sold people into slavery;
- -took land from Indians;
- -grew opium in India to ship into China, as various British merchants did;
- -turned a blind eye to sex-trafficking;
- -incited racial tension for political gain; and
- -voted for candidates who promised entitlement hand-outs even though those candidates disregarded the life of the unborn and favored the indoctrination of school children with sexual immorality.

Motivated by the GOSPEL, Bartolome' de Las Casas spent 60 years of his life fighting for the rights of native Americans, resulting in him being considered one of the first advocates for universal human rights.

Las Casas declared in his tract "Confesionario" that any Spaniard who refused to release his Indians would be denied forgiveness of sins.

Las Casas wrote "A brief report on the Destruction of the Indians" and "Apologetica historia de las Indias."

When these writings were translated and spread around Europe, an outrage arose pressuring the Spanish monarch, Charles V, to issue Leyes Nuevas (New Laws) in 1542, ordering an end to the enslavement and mistreatment of native Americans. This led to the liberating of thousands of indigenous Indians.

Bartolome' de Las Casas died July 17, 1566. He wrote:

> The main goal of divine Providence in the discovery of these tribes ... is ... the conversion and well-being of souls, and to this goal everything temporal must necessarily be directed.

Unfortunately, many GREED motivated plantation owners began to buy Africans from Arab Muslim slave markets and transport them to the New World.

∽

10. REFORMATION

At the time Spaniards were exploring the New World, a 34-year-old Augustinian monk named Martin Luther posted 95 debate questions or "theses" on the door of Wittenberg Church in the German Kingdom of Saxony on October 31, 1517.

This began the movement known as the Reformation. Luther's initial objection was to the methods employed by Johann Tetzel of selling indulgences to raise funds to rebuild the aging St. Peter's Basilica. Luther was fiercely opposed in public debates by Johann Eck.

In 1521, Martin Luther was summoned to stand trial before the most powerful man in the world, 21-year-old Catholic Holy Roman Emperor Charles V.

At the trial, called the Diet of Worms, Charles V initially dismissed Luther's theses as "an argument between monks." Luther was ordered to recant without his theses questions being addressed. He responded:

"Here I stand; I can do no other. God help me. Amen."

Luther was declared outside the protection of law. He was kidnapped and hid by Frederick III of Saxony in the Wartburg Castle, where he translated the New Testament into German. Luther gave his account:

> I greatly longed to understand Paul's Epistle to the Romans and nothing stood in the way but that one expression, "the justice of God," because I took it to mean that justice whereby God is just and deals justly in punishing the unjust.
>
> My situation was that, although an impeccable monk, I stood before God as a sinner troubled in conscience, and I had no confidence that my merit would assuage him.
>
> Therefore I did not love a just and angry God, but rather hated and murmured against him. Yet I clung to the dear Paul and had a great yearning to know that he meant ...

Luther continued:

> Night and day I pondered until I saw the connection between the justice of God and the statement "The just shall live by faith."
>
> Then I grasped that the justice of God is that righteousness by which through sheer grace and mercy God justifies us through faith.
>
> Thereupon I felt myself to be reborn and to have gone through open doors into paradise.
>
> The whole of Scripture took a new meaning, and whereas before "the justice of God" had filled me with hate, now it became inexpressibly sweet in greater love. This passage of Paul became to me a gate to heaven ...

Luther concluded:

> If you have a true faith that Christ is your Savior, then at once you have a gracious God, for faith leads you in and opens up God's heart

and will, that you should see pure grace and over-flowing love.

This it is to behold God in faith that you should look upon his fatherly, friendly heart, in which there is no anger nor ungraciousness.

He who sees God as angry does not see him rightly but looks only on a curtain, as if a dark cloud had been drawn across his face.

Luther, who died in 1546, stated:

If I profess with the loudest voice and clearest exposition every portion of the truth of God except precisely that little point which the world and the devil are at that moment attacking, I am not confessing Christ, however boldly I may be professing Christ.

Where the battle rages, there the loyalty of the soldier is proved and to be steady on all the battlefield besides is mere flight and disgrace if he flinches at that one point.

❧

11. JOHN WYCLIFFE & JAN HUS

Luther's world had been shaken by what happened a century earlier–the Great Schism, 1378-1417.

John Wycliffe (1330-1384) attempted a translation of Scriptures into English, for which he was declared a heretic and, after his death, had his bones burned.

The General Prologue of Wycliffe's 1384 translation of the Bible has the inscription:

The Bible is for the Government of the People, by the People, and for the People.

John Wycliffe influenced the Kingdom of Bohemia (present day Czech Republic). Its king, Charles IV, was the Holy Roman Emperor at that time, and his daughter, Anne, married England's King Richard II in 1382.

Bohemian scholars Professor Faulfash and Jerome

of Prague traveled to England and studied at Oxford. There they learned of Wycliffe's teachings, which they brought back to Bohemia. In Prague, the capital city of Bohemia, Jan Hus (1369-1415) enthusiastically embraced Wycliffe's teachings.

Hus boldly shared Scriptures translated into the Czech language. As a result, he was summoned to the Council of Constance. He was willing to recant, if his errors could be shown by Scripture, but instead, he was declared a heretic and burned at the stake.

Both Wycliffe and Hus lived before the invention of the printing press, whereas Martin Luther lived after.

∽

12. ROLE OF THE PRINTING PRESS

Mankind began "writing" around 3,300 BC, with the invention of cuneiform markings on clay tablets. Writing was then made on papyrus reeds from the Nile Delta, palm leaves, parchment from animal skins, strips of bamboo, and vellum from calfskin.

The Chinese developed the process of making paper from tree pulp or rags. Beginning in 175 AD, during the Han Dynasty, Chinese scholars placed paper over stone engravings of sayings of Confucius and made rubbings with charcoal.

This developed into laying paper over raised stone letters covered with ink, a technique which spread to other countries like Japan, where a Nara Empress printed a Buddhist charm in 768 AD.

Using a method with carved wooden or baked clay blocks, China, during the Tang Dynasty, created what could be considered the first "printed" book in 868 AD.

In China, Bi Sheng invented movable type printing with porcelain characters during the Song Dynasty, 1041, leading to China being the first to have printed "paper currency."

Printing of currency using copper plates occurred on a mass scale during Kublai Khan's Yuan Dynasty, 1215–1294, even being mentioned by Marco Polo.

Unfortunately, China over–printed its currency, leading to it being devalued. Inflation exploded as the currency depreciated by 1,000 percent. China became politically unstable and the Yuan Dynasty was overthrown in 1368.

The shear number of Chinese characters, though, over 50,000, discouraged China from making further printing innovations.

In 1234, Korea's Goryeo Dynasty invented the first "metal" movable type printing press. In 1443, Korean Emperor Sejong the Great introduced a 24–letter han'gul alphabet which made printing practical.

At nearly the same time, on the other side of the world, Johannes Gutenberg invented the western world's first "metal" movable type printing press.

Western civilization had long used a phonetic alphabet, dating back to a Semitic characters around 1500 BC. It was not until 1400 AD that Europeans began using carved wooden blocks, applied with ink, to print religious messages.

On August 24, 1455, Gutenberg printed his masterpiece, the Gutenberg Bible, regarded as the first book of significance ever printed. No longer copied tediously by hand and chained to pulpits, Bibles were soon mass produced.

Gutenberg, whose name means "beautiful mountain," wrote of his 42–line Gutenberg Bible, also called the Mazarin Bible, 1455:

> God suffers in the multitude of souls whom His word can not reach. Religious truth is imprisoned in a small number of manuscript books which confine instead of spread the public treasure.

Let us break the seal which seals up holy things and give wings to Truth in order that she may win every soul that comes into the world by her word no longer written at great expense by hands easily palsied, but multiplied like the wind by an untiring machine ...

Gutenberg continued:

Yes, it is a press, certainly, but a press from which shall flow in inexhaustible streams the most abundant and most marvelous liquor that has ever flowed to relieve the thirst of men.

Through it, God will spread His word; a spring of pure truth shall flow from it; like a new star it shall scatter the darkness of ignorance, and cause a light hithertofore unknown to shine among men.

In March of 1455, future Pope Pius II wrote in a letter to Cardinal Carvajal:

All that has been written to me about that marvelous man seen at Frankfurt is true. I have not seen complete Bibles but only a number of quires of various books of the Bible.

The script was very neat and legible, not at all difficult to follow – your grace would be able to read it without effort, and indeed without glasses.

Unfortunately for Gutenberg, he had borrowed 8,000 guilders from Johann Fust, who sued him at the archbishop's court in 1456 and took the print shop. Bankrupted, Gutenberg re-started a smaller print shop, and helped print Bibles in the town of Bamberg.

Mark Twain wrote in *A Tramp Abroad*, 1880:

We made a short halt at Frankfort–on–the–Main ... I would have liked to visit the birthplace of Gutenberg, but ... no memorandum of the house has been kept.

Gutenberg's invention was considered the most important event of the modern period as it began a printing revolution which significantly influenced Europe's Renaissance, Reformation, Age of Enlightenment, and the Scientific Revolution.

Over three centuries after the printing press was invented, Napoleon introduced it into Egypt when he invaded in 1798. On August 12, 1993, Pope John Paul II gave a rare copy of the Gutenberg Bible to President Bill Clinton at Denver's Regis University.

The word "Bible" comes from the Greek word 'biblia' meaning books. Since the invention of the printing press, the Holy Bible has been the most printed book in history, at an estimated 6 billion copies.

Victor Hugo wrote in *The Hunchback of Notre Dame*, 1831, book 5:

> The 15th century everything changes. Human thought discovers a mode of perpetuating itself ... Gutenberg's letters of lead ... supersede Orpheus's letters of stone ... The invention of printing is the greatest event in history. It is the mother of revolution ...

> Whether it be Providence or Fate, Gutenberg is the precursor of Luther.

❧

13. PROTESTANT REVOLT-ISLAMIC INVASION

As the Reformation spread, it unintentionally fueled a peasant uprising called the German Peasants' War in 1524. Mobs of poorly armed peasants threatened the aristocratic ruling class. The revolt was put down with over 100,000 peasants being slaughtered.

Meanwhile, in 1527, Charles V's unruly troops sacked Rome and imprisoned Pope Clement VII for six months. It was during his imprisonment that the Pope refused to annul the marriage between Charles V's aunt,

Catherine of Aragon, and England's King, Henry VIII.

Charles V began the Counter-Reformation and oversaw the Spanish colonization of the Americas, responding to the pleadings of Bartolome' de Las Casas by outlawing the enslavement of native Americans.

Spain used gold from the New World to fit out its army and navy to repel the Islamic invasion of Europe. In 1529, 35-year-old Suleiman the Magnificent sent 100,000 Muslim Turks to surround Vienna, Austria.

Martin Luther wrote (*Luther's Works–American Edition,* 55 volumes, Philadelphia: Fortress; St. Louis: Concordia, 1955–1986, vol. 46:170–171):

> The Turk is the rod of the wrath of the Lord our God ... If the Turk's god, the devil, is not beaten first, there is reason to fear that the Turk will not be so easy to beat ... Christian weapons and power must do it ...
>
> (The fight against the Turks) must begin with repentance, and we must reform our lives, or we shall fight in vain.
>
> (The Church should) drive men to repentance by showing our great and numberless sins and our ingratitude, by which we have earned God's wrath and disfavor, so that He justly gives us into the hands of the devil and the Turk.

As the Islamic threat intensified, reformer John Calvin wrote to Philip Melanchthon in 1543, (*Selected Works of John Calvin: Tracts & Letters,* I: 373):

> I hear of the sad condition of your Germany! ... The Turk again prepares to wage war with a larger force. Who will stand up to oppose his marching throughout the length and breadth of the land, at his mere will and pleasure?

In 1543, three years before his death, Martin Luther regrettably penned an anti-semitic work that contributed to future Jewish persecutions.

❧

14. PROTESTANT RIPPLE EFFECT

In the two centuries following Martin Luther and the start of the Protestant Reformation, kings in Europe chose different denominations for their kingdoms. This resulted in religious wars and millions migrating from one country to another for conscience sake.

In the 17th century, many religious refugees fled Europe to settle colonies in America. In her article "The Middle Colonies as the Birthplace of American Religious Pluralism," New York University Professor Emeritus Patricia Bonomi wrote: "The colonists were about 98 percent Protestant."

Of the 56 signers of the Declaration, most were Protestant, with the notable exception of Catholic Charles Carroll of Maryland. Samuel Adams stated when he signed the Declaration of Independence:

> This day, I trust, the reign of political protestantism will commence.

British Statesman Edmund Burke addressed Parliament, 1775:

> All Protestantism ... is a sort of dissent. But the religion most prevalent in our Northern Colonies is a refinement on the principle of resistance; it is the dissidence of dissent, and the protestantism of the Protestant religion.

John Adams wrote in *A Dissertation on the Canon and Feudal Law,* 1765:

> The desire of dominion ... when ... restraints are taken off ... becomes an encroaching, grasping, restless, and ungovernable power ... contrived by the great for the gratification of this passion ...
>
> Originally formed ... for the necessary defense ... against ... invasions ... yet ... tyranny,

cruelty, and lust ... was soon adopted by almost all the princes of Europe ... The people were held in ignorance ... till God in his benign providence raised up the champions who began and conducted the Reformation.

From the time of the Reformation to the first settlement of America, knowledge gradually spread in Europe, but especially in England; and in proportion as that increased and spread among the people ... tyranny ... lost ... strength.

Consistent with Adams' view is that of Robert D. Woodberry of the National University of Singapore, who wrote a paper titled "The Missionary Roots of Liberal Democracy" (*American Political Science Review*, Vol. 106, No. 2 May 2012).

Woodberry demonstrated statistically that countries where Protestant "conversionary" missionaries went in the 19th century became more prosperous in the 20th century, partly because these missionaries taught everyone to read so they could understand the Bible:

The association between Protestant missions and democracy is consistent in different continents and subsamples, and it is robust to more than 50 controls and to instrumental variable analyses.

On the importance of education, Luther wrote:

I am much afraid that schools will prove to be the great gates of hell unless they diligently labor in explaining the Holy Scriptures, engraving them in the hearts of youth.

I advise no one to place his child where the scriptures do not reign paramount. Every institution in which men are not increasingly occupied with the Word of God must become corrupt.

Luther added:

The Bible was written for men with a head upon their shoulders.

∽

15. ENGLAND'S HENRY VIII

The Reformation was brought to England by Henry VIII. He was married to Catherine of Aragon, daughter of Ferdinand and Isabella of Spain, who sent Columbus on his voyage. Catherine had previously been married to Henry's older brother Arthur for 6 months before he died in 1502. Catherine bore Henry a daughter, Mary I, but no son.

After 18 years, Henry began to make advances on Anne Boleyn, but she refused to be a mistresses. Henry sought an "annulment" from Catherine, insisting her previous marriage to his brother was not properly consummated. Pope Clement VII refused to grant the "annulment" on scriptural grounds, though it may have been influenced by the fact that Catherine's nephew was now the most powerful man in the world, Charles V of Spain, whose Spanish soldiers ransacked Rome and imprisoned Pope Clement for 6 months

Henry VIII broke from the Catholic Church and began the Church of England, declaring himself the head. The Archbishop of Canterbury, Thomas Crammer, nullified Henry's marriage to Catherine, allowing him to marry Anne Boleyn on January 25, 1533.

Anne disappointed Henry by not having a son, but a daughter, Elizabeth I, on September 7, 1533, After three miscarriages, Henry accused Anne of treason and she was beheaded on May 19, 1536.

In total, Henry VIII had six wives:

•Catherine of Aragon, divorced, (daughter was Mary I);

•Anne Boleyn, beheaded, (daughter was Elizabeth I);

•Jane Seymour, died, (son was Edward VI);

•Anne of Cleves, divorced (no children);

•Catherine Howard, beheaded (cousin of Anne Boleyn, no children);

•Catherine Parr, survived (no children by Henry VIII).

In 1534, the English Parliament passed the Act of Supremacy, giving Henry the title of "Supreme Head of the Church of England." All subjects were ordered to take an oath accepting this.

A Treason Act was passed making it a crime to write or speak anything that would accuse the King of heresy or tyranny. Many leaders in England fell out of favor and were arrested, as was Archbishop Woolsley, or executed, such as Sir Thomas More.

In 1536, Henry VIII was injured in a jousting accident. His health deteriorated and he developed a paranoid suspicion of subordinates. Eating primarily meat, he grew to 400 lbs. Suffering from gout and painful ulcerated open leg wounds, Henry died in 1547.

᪥

16. LIST OF 16TH CENTURY POPES

At this point, it may be helpful to see a list of Popes:

•Alexander VI, 1492–1503, known for dividing New World between Spain and Portugal with his Inter Caetera Bull of 1493.

•Pius III, September 22, 1503–October 18, 1503.

•Julius II, 1503–1513, who took control of all the Papal States for the first time and commissioned Michelangelo to paint the Sistine Chapel ceiling. He proposed the grand plan to rebuild the dangerously tilting St Peter's Basilica.

•Leo X, 1513–1521, was remembered for granting indulgences to those who donated to rebuild St. Peter's Basilica. He excommunicated Martin Luther in 1521, and extended the Spanish Inquisition into Portugal.

•Adrian VI, 1522–1523, had been the tutor of

Spain's Charles V. The only Dutch pope, he was the last non-Italian to be elected pope until Pope John Paul II in 1978.

•Clement VII, 1523–1534, was the cousin of earlier Pope Leo X. During his pontificate, Rome was plundered by Charles V's troops in 1527. He refused to recognized Henry VIII's divorce from Catherine of Aragon. He later crowned Charles V as Holy Roman Emperor at Bologna in 1530. Clement's niece was married to the future King of France, Henry II. He ordered Michelangelo to paint of The Last Judgment in the Sistine Chapel. In 1533, he heard for the first time the theory of Nicolaus Copernicus, that the center of the solar system was not the earth, but the sun.

•Paul III, 1534–1549, officially began the Counter-Reformation by opening the Council of Trent in 1545. His illegitimate son was the first Duke of Parma. He officially excommunicated Henry VIII in 1538, and appointed Michelangelo to supervise the rebuilding of St. Peter's Basilica in 1546.

•Julius III, 1550–1555, attempted to stop the spread of the Reformation by establishing the Collegium Germanicum in 1552, which was dedicated by Jesuit Saint Ignatius Loyola. He reconvened the Council of Trent. His reputation was tarnished by the scandal-ridden relationship with his adopted nephew, Innocenzo.

• Marcellus II, April 9, 1555–May 1, 1555.

•Paul IV, 1555–1559, was a member of the religious order of Theatines–dedicated to founding hospitals, practicing a modest lifestyle of virtue, reforming lax morals, and preaching the Gospel. He ordered Michelangelo to repaint coverings over the nude images in The Last Judgment painting. He required Catholic rulers to treat Protestant rulers as heretics, and he refused to recognize Elizabeth I as Queen of England.

•Pius IV, 1559–1565, reopened and closed the

Council of Trent, instituting the Tridentine Creed.

•Pius V, 1566–1572, previously held the position of Inquisitor of Como, and was so severe in his persecution of heretics that a city-wide rebellion erupted, forcing him to flee for his life. In 1570, he issued the Roman Missal, and officially excommunicated Queen Elizabeth I of England. During his pontificate, the Battle of Lepanto took place in 1571, after which he instituted the feast of Our Lady of Victory.

•Gregory XIII, 1572–1585, reformed the Julian calendar by creating the Gregorian Calendar in 1582. He strengthened diplomatic ties with Asia, and bestowed the Immaculate Conception as Patroness to the Philippine Islands with his bull Ilius Fulti Præsido in 1579.

•Sixtus V, 1585–1590, was a member of the Conventual Franciscan Order. He built several major basilicas in Rome, and limited the College of Cardinals, which holds papal elections, to 70.

•Urban VII, September 15–27, 1590, was the shortest–reigning pope. As trade ships began to bring tobacco purchased from native Americans into Europe, smoking became fashionable. He banned smoking in churches and instituted the first known worldwide smoking ban.

•Gregory XIV, 1590–1591, made gambling on papal elections punishable by excommunication.

•Innocent IX, October 29–December 3, 1591, supported Philip II of Spain's claim to England, and the Catholic League against Good King Henry Navarre during the French Wars of Religion.

17. SULTAN SULEIMAN THE MAGNIFICENT

From 1520 to 1566, Suleiman the Magnificent was the Sultan of the Ottoman Empire. His fleets dominated the Mediterranean Sea, the Red Sea, and the Persian Gulf. His armies invaded the Christian countries of Hungary, Serbia, and Austria. Suleiman annexed most of the Middle East, and huge areas of North Africa, including the Barbary States of Tripoli, Tunisia, Algeria, and Morocco.

The French political writer Montesquieu compared Ottoman Muslim despotism with Christian government in *The Spirit of the Laws,* 1748:

> A moderate Government is most agreeable to the Christian Religion, and a despotic Government to the Mahometan ...
>
> The Christian religion is a stranger to mere despotic power. The mildness so frequently recommended in the Gospel is incompatible with the despotic rage with which a prince punishes his subjects, and exercises himself in cruelty.
>
> As this religion forbids the plurality of wives, its princes are less confined, less concealed from their subjects, and consequently have more humanity: they are more disposed to be directed by laws, and more capable of perceiving that they cannot do whatever they please.
>
> While the Mahometan princes incessantly give or receive death, the religion of the Christians renders their princes ... less cruel. The prince confides in his subjects, and the subjects in the prince.
>
> How admirable the religion which, while it only seems to have in view the felicity of the other life, continues the happiness of this! ... It is the Christian religion that ... has hindered despotic power.

Montesquieu continued:

> From the characters of the Christian and Mahometan religions, we ought, without any further examination, to embrace the one and

reject the other: for it is much easier to prove that religion ought to humanize the manners of men than that any particular religion is true.

It is a misfortune to human nature when religion is given by a conqueror. The Mahometan religion, which speaks only by the sword, acts still upon men with that destructive spirit with which it was founded.

Sultan Suleiman the Magnificent defeated the Byzantines, Bulgars, Serbs, and in 1521, surrounded the city of Belgrade with 250,000 soldiers, bombarding it from an island in the Danube River. When Belgrade, one of Christendom's major cities, fell, panic spread throughout Europe. Suleiman deported Belgrade's entire Christian population to Istanbul as slaves.

In 1522, Suleiman attacked the Island of Rhodes with 400 ships and 100,000 troops. After a 5 month siege, the defenders capitulated and retreated to the Island of Malta.

To fully understand how seriously Europeans felt threatened by Suleiman, Martin Luther wrote in *On War Against the Turk* (1529):

> The Turk is the very devil incarnate ... The Turk fills heaven with Christians by murdering their bodies.

He wrote in *Preface to Book of Revelation* (1530):

> 2nd woe ... the 6th [evil] angel, the shameful Mohammed with his companions, the Saracens, who inflicted great plagues on Christendom, with his doctrine and with the sword.

In *Luther's Works* (3:121–122), he wrote:

> Yet it is more in accordance with the truth to say that the Turk is the Beast, because he is outside the church and openly persecutes Christ.

Luther wrote (*Tischreden,* 1532, Weimer, ed., 1, 330):

The Turk is the flesh of Antichrist ... (which)
slaughters bodily by the sword.

❧

18. CHARLES V'S ENEMIES

King Charles V of Spain, who was the Holy Roman
Emperor, was faced with multiple enemies, notably: 1)
Protestant Reformation; 2) Ottoman Turkish invasion;
and 3) France making a treaty with the Ottomans.

At the Battle of Pavia in 1525, the King of France,
Francis I, had his horse injured and was captured. He
was taken away to Madrid, Spain, where Charles V put
him in prison. Francis wrote in a letter to his mother:
"All is lost save honor."

After being forced to make concessions and
surrender territories, Francis I was released. Possibly
influencing his release was an ultimatum sent to Charles
V by the Ottoman Sultan Suleiman the Magnificent.

Shortly after his release, in 1526, Francis I began
negotiating a Franco–Ottoman Alliance with Sultan
Suleiman against Spain's King Charles V.

This alliance emboldened the Sultan to increase
his attack on Eastern European countries of Bulgaria,
Croatia, Bohemia, and Hungary. At the Battle of
Mohács in 1526, the Turks defeated the Hungarians
and killed their King Louis II. This was a shocking
moral defeat for all of Europe.

❧

19. FIRST SIEGE OF VIENNA

Emboldened by his victories, the 35-year-old Sultan
Suleiman laid siege to Vienna, Austria, in 1529. The
city was surrounded by an army of 100,000 Muslim
Turks. Miners tunneled under the city walls and suicide
bombers assaulted the gates of Vienna.

Miraculously, the city was saved by torrential

freezing rains which fell for weeks, resulting in sickness among Suleiman's troops. Some 10,000 of his supply camels sustained injuries from slipping on mud drenched roads. Suleiman abandoned the siege and returned to Constantinople to kill a relative who was challenging his throne. Before he left, he beheaded 4,000 Christian hostages.

In 1532, Suleiman again attempted to attack Vienna, but was turned back, resulting in him redirecting his attention to the east, attacking the Shi'a Muslims of Persia (Iran) in 1534.

In 1535, Charles V's General, the "Iron Duke" of Alba, won a significant victory against the Sultan at Tunis. This defeat motivated the Sultan to formalize his alliance with Francis I against Spain in 1536. This was the first time a European monarch officially made such an agreement with a Muslim power, resulting in calls for Francis I to be excommunicated.

France's Catholic King, as well as Europe's Protestant kings, considered the Turks as a check on Spain's power. The growing European political and religious disunity was to Suleiman's advantage.

❧

20. PERSIAN SAFAVID DYNASTY

As a result of the Franco–Ottoman Alliance, the Ottoman Turks forced Charles V to sign the humiliating Truce of Adrianople in 1547. This truce not only gave Turks control of Hungary, but required that the Turks be paid an enormous yearly tribute.

Charles V responded by joining with Hungary's King Ludwig II in seeking a Habsburg–Persian Alliance, as the Safavid Persian Empire was the Ottoman Empire's main enemy to the east.

Charles corresponded with Shah Ismail I, founder of Persia's Safavid dynasty, who ruled from 1501 to 1524.

Ismail I had embraced the Twelver version of Islam, acknowledging Twelve Imams as successors of Muhammad. Twelvers believed that the last Imam, Muhammad al-Mahdi, is hidden and will reappear as the promised Mahdi, ushering in the Second Coming of Jesus Christ (Isa), and together, they will kill all the Christians, Jews, apes and pigs.

Ismail I elevated Islamic clerics in authority, turning them into an aristocracy which continues to the present.

After Ismail I's death in 1524, Charles aligned himself with Ismail's son, Shah Tahmasp I. As a result of this alliance, whenever the Ottoman Empire attacked westward into Europe, Persia would attack the Ottoman Empire from the east. An Ottoman–Safavid Persian War erupted from 1532 to 1555.

Charles V briefly allied himself with England's Henry VIII in 1543, and together they forced France to sign the Truce of Crepy-en-Laonnois.

When Shah Tahmasp died in 1576, his son, Haydar Mirza, declared himself Shah. His half-sister, Pari Khan Khanum, betrayed him, resulting in his being murdered by his brother, Ismail II.

Ismail II had been imprisoned for 20 years where he was almost murdered by supporters of Haydar Mirza.

As Shah, Ismail II attempted to move Persia back to the Sunni version of Islam. When he treated his half-sister, Pari Khan Khanum, wrongly, she arranged for him to be poisoned by one of his concubines in 1577.

Pari Khan Khanum ruled Persia for two years, until the older, blind, and pleasure seeking Mohammad Khodabanda was appointed Shah.

Mohammad Khodabanda's wife, Mahd-e Olya, manipulated her way into control and had Pari Khan Khanum strangled to death. From behind the throne, Mahd-e Olya effectively ruled Persia from 1578 to 1587.

Persia's internal dissension emboldened the Turks to attack, beginning another Ottoman–Safavid Persian War, from 1578 to 1590. The elder son of Mohammed Khodabanda and his wife, Mahd-e Olya, was Hamza Mirza. He attempted to seize control of Persia in 1586, but was suspiciously murdered.

In 1587, Mohammed Khodabanda's younger son, Abbas I, dethroned his father and became Shah. He hated the Sunni version of Islam and required all Persians to embrace Shiism.

∽

21. LIST OF PERSIAN SHAHS

A list of Shahs of the Safavid Persian Empire are:
- Shah Ismail I (reigned 1501–1524);
- Shah Tahmap I (reigned 1524–1576);
- Shah Ismail II (reigned 1576–1577);
- Shah Mohammed Khodabanda (reigned 1578–1587);
- Shah Abbas I (reigned 1588–1629);
- Shah Safi (reigned 1629–1642);
- Shah Abbas II (reigned 1642–1666);
- Shah Suleiman (reigned 1666–1694); and
- Shah Sultan Husayn (reigned 1694–1722), overthrown, last Shah of the Safavid Dynasty.

∽

22. ANGLO-PERSIAN ALLIANCE

Though the British Crown sought trade and favorable ties with the Ottoman Empire against Spain, English merchants Sir Anthony Sherley and his brother Robert Sherley arrived in Persia seeking trade in 1598.

They initiated an Anglo–Persian Alliance, as Persia wanted help against the Ottoman Empire, its main enemy to the west.

The Sherley brothers advised Shah Abbas I on how

to upgrade his military and modernize his royal cavalry. They assisted in training his army, which consisted mostly of captured "Ghulam" slave soldiers from Armenia, Georgia, Circassia, and other Caucasians.

Robert Sherley married a Christianize Circassian woman from Shah Abbas' court, who took the name Lady Teresa Sampsonia. She is considered by some as the first Persian to travel to England.

Persia's first diplomatic mission to Europe was sent by Abbas in 1599, traveling through Moscow, Norway, Germany, Rome, where they met Pope Clement VIII, and finally to Spain in 1602, during the reign of Philip III.

A Persian who accompanied Anthony Sherley in his travels was Uluch Beg. In Spain, he converted to Catholicism and was referred to as Don Juan of Persia. He wrote of his experiences in a book published in 1604.

Persia's Shah Abbas greatly wanted Spain's help in fighting the Ottoman Empire, and was even being willing to grant trading rights and permission for Christianity to be preached in Persia.

King Philip III of Spain, however, had inherited the Portuguese Empire and wanted the Portuguese port of Hormuz. He wanted the Shah to end relations with the British East India Company, and insisted the Shah make all 400,000 of his Christian Armenian subjects embrace Catholicism. These stipulations ended all negotiations.

Meanwhile, Europeans became fascinated with the Persian Shah, with even Shakespeare making reference to him in the play *Twelfth Night*, 1601–1602.

Anthony and Robert Sherley's military advice was instrumental in Shah Abbas' victories over the Turks in yet another Ottoman–Safavid Persian War, 1603–1618.

When the Christian Kingdom of Kakheti appealed to the Ottoman Empire for help, the Persian Shah retaliated by killing or deporting two-thirds of their population.

Shah Abbas I devastated the Christian Georgian city of Tblisi, killing 70,000 Kakheti Georgian peasants. He deported another 200,000 Georgian captives to Persia, where he had the Georgian queen Ketevan tortured to death for not renouncing Christianity.

Beginning in 1604, he forcibly resettled 300,000 Christian Armenians from their homeland, with thousands dying en route, to an area near his new capital of Isfahan.

The Anglo–Persian Alliance gave the British East India Company an open door to trade with Persia, allowing English access to the silk trade though Jask in the Strait of Hormuz in 1616.

Abbas I drove the Portuguese from their bases in the Persian Gulf. In 1602, he expelled the Portuguese out of Bahrain, and with the help of 4 English ships, Abbas captured Hormuz from the Portuguese in 1622.

Shah Abbas I fought the Muslim leaders of northern India over control of Kandahar in Afghanistan, during the Mughal–Safavid Persian War of 1622–1623.

Abbas I had five sons. Two died in childhood and three survived to adulthood. Abbas became paranoid that his eldest son might be conspiring to dethrone him, as he had done to his father, Mohammed Khodabanda.

His suspicions increased when, on a royal hunt, the son broke protocol by killing a boar before the Shah. Abbas arranged for his son to be murdered in 1615.

Concerned that the next son was conspiring for the throne, Abbas had him blinded in 1621, then murdered. Abbas had his last son blinded and imprisoned in 1627.

In 1629, Abbas designated a grandson, Shah Safi, to be his successor. Shah Safi ruthlessly killed anyone he became suspicious of. He indulged in wine and opium, but hated tobacco so much that anyone caught smoking tobacco had molten lead poured down his throat.

Another Ottoman–Safavid Persian War raged from 1623 to 1639, but this time the Ottomans prevailed.

Shah Safi's excessive drinking led to his death in 1642, being succeeded by 9-year-old Shah Abbas II. Three years later, the Grand Vizer (Prime Minister) was suspiciously murdered. Young Shah Abbas II, now age 12, ordered all those involved to be executed.

In 1649, Abbas II captured Kandahar, Afghanistan, from northern India's Mughal Emperor Shah Jahan, who was known for building the Taj Mahal and for his efforts to exterminate the Sikhs.

Abbas II fought Russia's Ivan IV "The Terrible" in the Russo–Persian War of 1651–1653.

In 1652, the Dutch East India Company sent ambassador Joan Cuneaus to Persia to meet with Abbas II, who received him cordially, even allowing him to drink from the Shah's wine chalice.

Shah Abbas II died in 1666, being succeeded by 18 year old Shah Suleiman I. Having the Islamic name for Solomon, Shah Suleiman I was preoccupied with his harem, leaving government business to his grand vizers.

When the Turks were defeated at the Battle of Vienna in 1683, Shah Suleiman I refused alliances with European countries which would have allowed him to take advantage of the Ottoman Empire's weakness.

In 1668, Shah Suleiman requested artisans from William of Orange, the Stadtholder of Holland, who later became King William III of England.

In 1687, the Danish East India Company captured a Bengali ship off the coast of India carrying goods belonging to Armenian merchants who lived in Persia.

Shah Suleiman I sent a diplomat to the Danish capital of Copenhagen in 1691, requesting payment, presenting a list of the goods taken and the names of the

Armenian merchants to whom they belonged. To the diplomat's disappointment, no payments were made.

Dying in 1694, partly due to heavy drinking, Suleiman let his eunuchs pick the next Shah, saying if they wanted peace and quiet they should pick the elder son, but if they wanted to make the empire more powerful, they should pick the younger.

They picked the elder, Sultan Husayn, who became the Safavid dynasty's last Shah, being overthrown in 1722.

❧

23. WESTERN EUROPEAN UPHEAVALS

Western Europe faced internal and external upheavals from the Protestant Reformation on one hand and Ottoman Turkish attacks on the other.

Protestant Reformer John Calvin wrote in *Sermons on Timothy & Titus*:

> The Turks at this day, can allege and say for themselves: "We serve God from our ancestors!" – It is a good while since Mahomet gave them the cup of his devilish dreams to drink, and they got drunk with them.
>
> It is about a thousand years since cursed hellhounds were made drunk with their follies – Let us be wise and discreet! – For otherwise, we shall be like the Turks and Heathen.

Calvin wrote in *Commentary of 2nd Thessalonians:*

> Since Mohammed was an apostate, he turned his followers, the Turks, from Christ ... The sect of Mohammed was like a raging overflow, which in its violence tore away about half of the Church.

John Calvin wrote in *Commentary on Daniel*:

> Turks have spread far and wide, and the world is filled with impious despisers of God.

John Calvin wrote in *Institutes of the Christian*

Religion (Book II, Chapter VI):

> For even if many men once boasted that they worshiped ... the Maker of heaven and earth, yet because they had no Mediator it was not possible for them truly to taste God's mercy, and thus be persuaded that he was their Father ...

> So today the Muslim Turks, although they proclaim at the top of their lungs that the Creator of heaven and earth is God, still, while repudiating Christ, substitute an idol in place of the true God.

❧

24. PEACE OF AUGSBURG

Reformers who "protested" certain Catholic doctrines were referred to as "Protestants" or "Reformed." These included: Martin Luther, John Calvin, Thomas Crammer, John Knox, Philip Melanchthon, William Tyndale, and Huldrych Zwingli.

In 1545, during the reign of Holy Roman Emperor Charles V of Spain, the Council of Trent officially began the Catholic Counter–Reformation. Protestant European kings broke away from the Catholic Holy Roman Empire, and consequently refused to help Spain defend Europe against the Turks, and in some cases even made treaties with the Turks.

In 1538, Turkish Admiral Hayreddin Babarossa of Algiers defeated the Catholic Holy League, led by Italian Admiral Andrea Doria, at the Battle of Preveza.

In 1541, Spanish conquistador Cortés returned to Spain after conquering Mexico, and he joined Andrea Doria's fleet in fighting the Turks.

As Ottoman aggression increased, Charles V felt pressured to negotiate with Protestant German kings. In an attempt to reunite the Holy Roman Empire against the Turks, Charles V agreed to a truce at Nuremberg. Eric

W. Gritisch wrote in *Martin-God's Court Jester: Luther in Retrospect* (Philadelphia: Fortress, 1983, p. 69):

> Afraid of losing the much-needed support of the German princes for the struggle against the Turkish threat from the south, Emperor Charles V agreed to a truce between Protestant and Catholic territories in Nuremberg in 1532 ...

> Thus the Lutheran movement was, for the first time, officially tolerated and could enjoy a place in the political sun of the Holy Roman Empire.

Then, on September 25, 1555, Charles V signed the monumental Peace of Augsburg. This treaty contained a little Latin phrase that had enormous repercussions – "curios regio eius religio," which meant "whose is the reign his is the religion." In other words, each king could decide what would be believed in his kingdom, as long as they agreed to work together to stop the Islamic invasion into Europe.

A month later, October 25, 1555, Charles V, suffering from severe gout, possibly from his diet of mostly meat, began abdicating his throne. In 1556, he secluded himself in the monastery of Yuste where he died in 1558. His son Philip II ruled in his stead.

◆

25. SULEIMAN THE LAWGIVER

Suleiman was also called "the Lawgiver," as wherever he conquered, he forced subdued Christian populations to follow burdensome laws. They had to pay the holders of the timars (lords of the fiefdom) a tenth of the produce from the ground, though often by abuse, this was a higher percent.

They were required to render compulsory or villein (serf tied to the land) service. They paid heavy rents and taxes, such as: poll tax, bride tax, hoof tax, pasture tax, bee tax, mill tax, herd tax, meadow tax. They had to provide provisions for the Turkish army taking the field. They even were forced to deliver up a tenth of their boys for service in the Sultan's army. The consequences of not complying with these laws were fines, imprisonment, slavery, torture, and death.

Suleiman's pirates raided European coasts. Ohio State University Professor Robert C. Davis wrote *Christian Slaves, Muslim Masters: White Slavery in the Mediterranean, the Barbary Coast and Italy 1500–1800* (Palgrave Macmillian, 2003).

In 1544, Algerian pirates carried away so many Europeans into slavery from the Bay of Naples, over 7,000, that the price of a slave in the slave markets of North Africa dropped to where one could "swap a Christian for an onion."

In 1554, Muslim pirates sacked Vieste in southern Italy and took 6,000 captives.

◆

26. CATHOLIC MISSIONARIES

In 1540, St. Ignatius of Loyola founded the Compania (Company or Society of Jesus).

The next year, in 1541, St. Francis Xavier led a small group from Libson, Portugal, to be missionaries to the Far East, traveling to Mozambique, India, Malacca, Maluku Islands, Amboina, Ternate, China and Japan.

Xavier arrived in Japan in 1549, and through his ministry, the powerful daimyo (lord) Ōmura Sumitada was baptized, followed by 300,000 becoming Christian by the end of the 16th century.

Succeeding generations brought severe persecution to these "Hidden Christians," called Kakure Kirishitan, also called "Ancient Christians" or Mukashi Kirishitan. Martin Scorsese's movie *SILENCE* (2016) gave their account. Nagasaki became the most Christian city in all of Japan, until it was tragically devastated during

World War II by the dropping of the atomic bomb.

In 1556, Dominican Gaspar da Cruz was the first modern missionary to reach Guangzhou, China. He wrote the first complete book describing the Ming Dynasty.

Portuguese Jesuit missionary Bento de Góis, dressed as an Armenian merchant, became the first European to travel overland from India, across Afghanistan, through the Pamirs, to arrive in China in 1598. Unfortunately, Saracen Muslims raided the caravan he was traveling with and destroyed his meticulously kept travel journal.

Matteo Ricci was an Italian Jesuit scholar and missionary, from 1582 to 1610, to Portuguese Macau and China. He was the first European to enter the Forbidden City of Beijing and visit the imperial Ming palace. He became an expert in Chinese language and culture. The Wanli emperor respected him for his knowledge of science, astronomy, and map making skill.

In 1602, Ricci published the *Kunyu Wanguo Quantu* – the first world map in Chinese. Ricci made several notable coverts among the Chinese ruling class. He was later criticized by novice missionaries for having embraced the Chinese culture too much.

In 1624, the Portuguese Jesuit missionary António de Andrade was the first European to cross the Himalayas and reach Tibet.

In 1626, Portuguese Jesuit missionaries Estêvão Cacella with João Cabral were the first Europeans to reach Bhutan, a small country along the China Silk Road, bordered by Tibet to the north and India to the south.

Catholic missionaries accompanied the Spanish expeditions to America, including those of Narvaez 1527–1528, and De Soto, 1539–1542. At least 15 priests lost their lives attempting to evangelize native tribes.

Catholic missionaries arrived in Brazil in 1540.

In 1549, missionary Luis Cancer served as the Dominican apostle of Guatemala.

In 1569, priests with Father Rogel worked in South Carolina among the Orista tribe and on the Spanish post of Santa Elena.

In 1570, Father Segura, Father Luis de Quiros and seven novices and lay brothers undertook a mission among the Powhatan Indians in Virginia. They met friendly Indians and built a log chapel. The next year they were massacred.

In 1577, Father Pedro Martinez landed with a small party on Cumberland Island on the Georgia coast, was attacked and murdered by the savages. Father Juan Rogel and Brother Francisco de Villareal worked among the Calusa tribe in southern Florida.

Father Antonio Sedeno and Brother Domingo Baez began the first Georgia mission on St. Simon's Island Georgia among the Yamasee tribe.

In 1577, Father Alonso de Reynoso and several Franciscans began work with the Timucua and Yamasee tribes near St. Augustine, Florida. In 1597, natives attacked and killed many of them.

Missionaries arrived in Paraguay in 1587.

✁

27. SIEGE OF MALTA

In 1565, Sultan Suleiman the Magnificent dominated the Mediterranean. He had intentions of not only capturing Sicily, Sardinia, Majorca, and southern Spain, but invading Rome itself. The only thing standing in his way was the small rocky Island of Malta just south of Sicily, defended by the Knights of Malta.

In March of 1565, Sultan Suleiman the Magnificent sent Algerian Admiral Turgut Reis to Malta with 200 ships and 40,000 Muslim soldiers, including 6,500 elite Janissary troops. Dragut stated:

Unless you have smoked out this nest of vipers, you can do no good anywhere.

Queen Elizabeth I of England reportedly remarked:

If the Turks should prevail against the Isle of Malta, it is uncertain what further peril might follow to the rest of Christendom.

The 500 Knights of Malta, with some 5,500 soldiers and inhabitants, were led by 70 year old Jean Parisot de Valette. Pleas for reinforcements went out across Europe, but since defense seemed futile, few responded.

La Valette addressed his men:

A formidable army composed of audacious barbarians is descending on this island. These persons, my brothers, are enemies of Jesus Christ.

Today, it is a question of the defense of our faith–as to whether the Gospels are to be superseded by the Koran. God on this occasion demands of us our lives, already vowed to his service. Happy will be those who first consummate this sacrifice.

The Turks attacked again and again, reducing one of their fortresses to rubble, but the Knights kept fighting, resolved to save Western Civilization.

Finally, after nearly two month of fighting, Dragut was killed and the Muslim navy sailed away on September 11, 1565. The Sultan vowed retaliation.

⤸

28. MEDITERRANEAN

In 1566, Turks attacked Granada, capturing 4,000 men, women and children. In the Muslim slave markets it was said to be "raining Christians in Algiers."

In the same year, Turks and Corsairs sailed up the Adriatic coast and landed at Fracaville, resulting in residents abandoning over 500 square miles of coastline. Turks captured the Island of Gozo and carried away the entire population of 5,000 into slavery.

On August 3, 1571, Ottoman Turks, under the command of Lala Kara Mustafa Pasha, surrounded the Christians in Famagusta, Cyprus.

The Christian defenders were promised safe passage to leave if they surrendered. Lala Kara Mustafa Pasha broke his promise by demanding a boy for his pederasty. When the Venetian commander, Marco Antonio Bragadin, refused, the Muslim leader became furious and flayed Bragadin alive.

Turkish warriors then killed all 6,000 Christians prisoners. The beautiful St. Nicholas Church was turned into the Lala Mustafa Pasha Mosque.

After this, Turkish Muslims ravaged Italian coasts and leveled towns in Sicily. They planned to attack Rome and from there conquer the rest of western Europe.

❧

29. LIST OF TURKISH SULTANS

At this point, it may be helpful to see a list of the Ottoman Empire Sultans during this period:

- Mehmed II "The Conqueror," was Sultan 1451–1481, conquering Constantinople;
- Bayezid II was Sultan from 1481 till his abdication in 1512;
- Selim I was Sultan 1512–1520;
- Suleiman I "The Magnificent" was Sultan 1520–1566, attacking on land, laying siege as far as Vienna, and at sea besieging the Island of Malta;
- Selim II "The Drunkard" was Sultan 1566–1574, fighting the Battle of Lepanto;
- Murad III was Sultan 1574–1595;
- Mehmed III was Sultan 1595–1603;
- Ahmed I was Sultan 1603–1617;

- Mustafa I "The Mad" was Sultan 1617–1618, being deposed for mental instability. He was Sultan again 1622–1623, till deposed again;
- Osman II was Sultan 1618–1622, deposed during Janissary riot and murdered by Grand Vizier Kara Davud Pasha;
- Murad IV "Conqueror of Baghdad" was Sultan 1623–1640. His pirates raided England, capturing thousands, including one of the Pilgrims' ships;
- Ibrahim, "The Mad" or "Conqueror of Crete" was Sultan 1640–1648. He was deposed in coup and strangled to death by orders of Grand Vizier Mevlevî Mehmed Pasha;
- Mehmed IV "The Hunter" was Sultan 1648–1687. He was deposed after his defeat at Second Battle of Mohács;
- Suleiman II "The Warrior" was Sultan 1687–1691;
- Ahmed II "The Warrior Prince" was Sultan 1691–1695;
- Mustafa II "The Warrior" was Sultan 1695–1703, being deposed in a Janissary uprising, called "the Edirne Event."

❧

30. BATTLE OF LEPANTO

After Suleiman the Magnificent died, his son, Selim II, became Sultan, being nicknamed "the Drunkard" for his notorious reputation for debauchery.

As Islamic invasion threatened Rome, Pope Pius V called Europe to pray, and he assembled a Holy League of the Christian states of Spain, Naples, Sicily, Venice, Genoa, Sardinia, Savoy, Tuscany, Urbino, Papal States, Germans, Croatians, and the Knights of Malta.

The Holy League was led by 24-year-old Don John of Austria, the illegitimate son of Emperor Charles V and the half brother of King Philip II of Spain. Gold from the New World was used to fit out Spain's navy to keep the Muslims from taking over the Mediterranean.

The Battle of Lepanto took place on October 7, 1571, in the Gulf of Patras, off the western coast of Greece. It was the largest battle on the Mediterranean, and the last major sea battle fought primarily with rowing vessels. The Holy League had 12,920 sailors, 43,000 rowers, and 28,000 Spanish, German and Italian fighting troops in 206 galleys and 6 galleasses.

The Turkish fleet was led by Ali Pasha, who served under Sultan Selim II. It consisted of 230 galleys and 56 galliots, carrying 82,000 sailors and soldiers, powered by thousands of Christian galley slaves rowing under the decks. Ali Pasha was joined by the corsair pirates Chulouk Bey of Alexandria and Uluj Ali.

The morning of the battle, the Holy League was at a great disadvantage, rowing against the wind. Don John led his men on deck in a prayer. Suddenly the wind changed 180 degrees to favor the Holy League, whose ships then collided into Ali Pasha's fleet. The fierce fighting lasted five hours.

Don John sailed his flagship, *Real*, into Ali Pasha's flagship. Ali Pasha was finally killed and his head was hung from the ship. The Ottomans lost 25,000 soldiers and all but 30 of their ships. The Holy League lost 12 galleys and 13,000 men, but freed 15,000 Christian galley slaves from Muslim ships.

It was a crushing defeat for the Turks. The Battle of Lepanto is considered by many historians to be the most decisive naval battle since the Battle of Actium of 31 BC. Pope Pius V instituted the feast day of Our Lady of Victory to commemorate the battle.

Had the Muslims not been defeated, they would have invaded Italy and possibly conquered Europe.

31. G.K. CHESTERTON'S POEM

To commemorate the battle, English author G.K. Chesterton wrote the poem "Lepanto," in 1911:

... St. Michael's on his Mountain in the sea–roads of the north,

(Don John of Austria is girt and going forth.)

Where the grey seas glitter and the sharp tides shift,

And the sea–folk labor and the red sails lift.

He shakes his lance of iron and he claps his wings of stone;

The noise is gone through Normandy; the noise is gone alone ...

Don John calling through the blast and the eclipse,

Crying with the trumpet, with the trumpet of his lips,

Trumpet that sayeth ha!

Domino gloria!

Don John of Austria is shouting to the ships.

King Philip's in his closet with the Fleece about his neck,

(Don John of Austria is armed upon the deck) ...

And death is in the phial and the end of noble work,

But Don John of Austria has fired upon the Turk ...

Gun upon gun, ha! ha! Gun upon gun, hurrah!

Don John of Austria has loosed the cannonade,

The Pope was in his chapel before day of battle broke,

(Don John of Austria is hidden in the smoke) ...

He sees as in a mirror on the monstrous twilight sea,

The crescent of his cruel ships whose name is mystery;

They fling great shadows foe–wards, making Cross and Castle dark,

They veil the plumed lions on the galleys of St. Mark;

And above the ships are palaces of brown, black–
bearded chiefs,

And below the ships are prisons, where with
multitudinous griefs,

Christian captives sick and sunless, all a laboring race
repines,

Like a race in sunken cities, like a nation in the mines.

They are lost like slaves that swat, and in the skies of
morning hung,

The stairways of the tallest gods when tyranny was young.

They are countless, voiceless, hopeless as those fallen
or fleeing on,

Before the high Kings' horses in the granite of Babylon.

And many a one grows witless in his quiet room in hell,

Where a yellow face looks inward through the lattice
of his cell,

And he finds his God forgotten, and he seeks no more
a sign –

But Don John of Austria has burst the battle–line!

Don John pounding from the slaughter–painted poop,

Purpling all the ocean like a bloody pirate's sloop,

Scarlet running over on the silvers and the golds,

Breaking of the hatches up and bursting of the holds,

Thronging of the thousands up that labor under sea,

White for bliss and blind for sun and stunned for liberty.

Vivat Hispania! Domino Gloria!

Don John of Austria has set his people free!

Cervantes on his galley sets the sword back in the sheath,

Don John of Austria rides homeward with a wreath.

And he sees across a weary land a straggling road in
Spain,

Up which a lean and foolish knight forever rides in vain,

And he smiles, but not as Sultans smile, and settles back the blade ...

But Don John of Austria rides home from the Crusade.

Hilaire Belloc wrote in *The Great Heresies* (1938):

> This violent Mohammedan pressure on Christendom from the East made a bid for success by sea as well as by land.
>
> The last great Turkish organization working now from the conquered capital of Constantinople, proposed to cross the Adriatic, to attack Italy by sea and ultimately to recover all that had been lost in the Western Mediterranean.
>
> There was one critical moment when it looked as though the scheme would succeed. A huge Mohammedan armada fought at the mouth of the Gulf of Corinth against the Christian fleet at Lepanto. The Christians won that naval action and the Western Mediterranean was saved.
>
> But it was a very close thing, and the name of Lepanto should remain in the minds of all men with a sense of history as one of the half dozen great names in the history of the Christian world.

᪥

32. *MIGUEL DE CERVANTES*

One of the better known participants in the Battle of Lepanto was Miguel de Cervantes (1547–1616), the author who published *Don Quixote de La Mancha,* in 1605, considered the first modern European novel.

Miquel de Cervantes was wounded in the battle and lost the use of his left hand. Four years later, on his trip home, he was captured by Muslim Barbary pirates and spent five years as a slave in Algiers. He was finally ransomed by the Catholic Order of Trinitarians and returned to Madrid, Spain. He described this in a semi-autobiographical chapter:

> They put a chain on me ... I passed my life in that bano with several other gentlemen and persons of quality marked out as held to ransom; but though at times, or rather almost always, we suffered from hunger and scanty clothing, nothing distressed us so much as hearing and seeing at every turn the unexampled and unheard–of cruelties my master inflicted upon the Christians.

> Every day he hanged a man, impaled one, cut off the ears of another; and all with so little provocation, or so entirely without any, that the Turks acknowledged he did it merely for the sake of doing it, and because he was by nature murderously disposed towards the whole human race.

In *Don Quixote de La Mancha*, Cervantes described how Barbary raiders would attack Christian areas of the Mediterranean. If they were captured, they would say they wanted to become Christian, resulting in their release. After being freed, though, they would revert back to being raiders:

> Some obtain these testimonials with good intentions, others put them to a cunning use; for when they go to pillage on Christian territory, if they chance to be cast away, or taken prisoners, they produce their certificates and say that from these papers may be seen the object they came for, which was to remain on Christian ground, and that it was to this end they joined the Turks in their foray ...

> In this way they escape the consequences of the first outburst and make their peace with the Church before it does them any harm, and then when they have the chance they return to Barbary to become what they were before.

As Martin Luther influenced the development of

the German language, and as William Shakespeare influenced the English language, Miguel de Cervantes influenced the Spanish language.

Miguel de Cervantes and William Shakespeare died on the same day, April 23, 1616, though some claim a day earlier. In fact, it was at least eleven days earlier, as Catholic Spain used the Gregorian Calendar and Anglican England still used the old Julian Calendar.

ఌ

33. GREGORIAN CALENDAR

March was the first month of the year for millennia, as ancient peoples used various lunar calendars based on the cycles of the moon. These calendars were difficult to reconcile with each other.

In 45 BC, Julius Caesar wanted all the countries conquered by Rome to used a unified solar–based calendar. This is called the "Julian Calendar."

Caesar was, in a sense, the first globalist. His successor, August Caesar, also sought worldwide domination, even conducting the first empire–wide census to count everyone under his control– an early precursor to today's NSA government tracking.

Remnants of "March" being the first month of the calendar year can be seen in the old Roman Latin names:

- •September – "Sept" is Latin for seven;
- •October – "Oct" is Latin for eight (ie. octogon=eight sided);
- •November – "Nov" is Latin for nine; and
- •December – "Dec" is Latin for ten (ie. decimal=divisible by ten).

Rome's old fifth month, Quintilis, was renamed "July" after Julius Caesar. As it only had 30 days, Caesar took a day from the old end of the year, February, and added it to July, giving the month 31 days.

The next emperor, Augustus Caesar, renamed the old sixth month, Sextilis, after himself, calling it "August." He also took a day from the old end of the year, February, and added it to August, giving that month 31 days, and leaving February with only 28 days.

The Julian Calendar inserted a leap day to February every 4th year. By 1582, it became clear that the Julian Calendar was slightly inaccurate by about 11 minutes per year. This resulted in the calculation tables, used to determine the date of Easter since the time of Constantine, were ten days off.

Constantine, at the Council of Nicea in 325 AD, ended the practice of asking Jewish rabbis when Passover would be each year, and instead instituted a new formula to determine the date of Easter – the first Sunday after the first full moon after the Spring Equinox.

In 1582, Pope Gregory XIII revised the calendar by eliminating ten days and setting a leap year every 4th year, except for years divisible by 100, unless that year is also divisible by 400.

It sounds complicated, but it is so accurate that the Gregorian Calendar is still in use internationally today. It was quickly adopted in Catholic countries, but Eastern Orthodox countries and Protestant countries, like Queen Elizabeth I's England, continued to use the old Julian Calendar.

To distinguish between the two calendars, dates were recorded as "OS" for "Old Style" and "NS" for "New Style." England reluctantly waited until 1752 to adopt the Gregorian Calendar.

As England, France, Holland, Spain, Portugal, and other Christian European countries set up colonies around the world, the Gregorian Calendar came to be used globally. Because of this, all dates in the world came to be designated as either BC "Before Christ" or AD "Anno Domini" – in the Year of the Lord's Reign.

34. HOLY LEAGUE DISUNITY

After defeating the Ottoman navy at the Battle of Lepanto, the Holy League fell into disunity. Instead of following up on their victory and freeing the Mediterranean coasts, Greek Islands, and Constantinople, from Muslim control, the opportunity was lost. Spain decided to send its armies and navy to smash the Protestant Reformation in Holland and England.

Within six months, the Ottomans rebuilt their navy and added eight of the largest ships ever seen in the Mediterranean.

Nevertheless, they had lost so many experienced sailors at the Battle of Lepanto, the Turks avoided confrontations with Christians. An Islamic maxim of warfare is, when your enemy is strong – retreat; when your enemy is weak – attack.

Just as a century earlier, when Turks took advantage of the political rivalry between Italian city–states of Venice and Genoa, to advance upon Constantinople, in like manner, after Holy League disunity, Ottomans retook the important city of Tunis from Spanish control in 1574, and defeated the Portuguese, recapturing Fez, Morocco, in 1579.

Ottomans now controlled the majority of the Mediterranean coast, from the Strait of Gibraltar to Croatia and Slovenia, with the exception of a few strategic Spanish and Portuguese posts.

Other major battles against the Turks were the Battle of Vienna on September 11, 1683, and the Battle of Zenta on September 11, 1697. An in depth look at the 1,400 year Islamic expansion is in the book *What Every American Needs to Know about the Qur'an–A History of Islam & the United States.*

35. RUSSIA

Novgorod was the first and only Russian Republic until modern times. Founded as a Viking trading post near the Baltic Sea in 859 AD, it is considered the first capital of the Kievan Rus' people, cultural ancestors of Belarus, Russia, and Ukraine. In 882, Oleg moved the capital to the city of Kiev.

During the Middle Ages, Novgorod grew so prosperous that was it was Russia's second main city after Kiev. It controlled an enormous area as large as Sweden. Novgorod's economy was based on Baltic sea trade, being a member of the Hansa Union of rich Baltic ports. It was situated on one of the main travel routes from Northern Europe to Rome and Constantinople.

During this era, Russia was divided into numerous princedoms which fought against each other. Novgorod threw its support behind Vladimir the Great of Kiev.

In 986 AD, Vladimir decided to throw his pagan gods in the Dnieper River and embrace monotheism. He was soon visited by some Bulgar Muslims from Khwarezm, who invited him to adopt Islam. *The Primary Chronicle,* the official record of Russia from 850 AD to 1110 AD, compiled in Kiev in 1113, reported:

> They replied that they believed in Allah, and that Mohammed instructed them to practice circumcision, to eat no pork, to drink no wine, and after death, promised them complete fulfillment of their carnal desires. "Mohammed," they asserted, "will give each man 70 fair women. He may choose one fair one, and upon that woman will Mohammed confer the charms of them all, and she shall be his wife." Mohammed promises that one may then satisfy every desire. But whoever is poor in this world will be no different in the next."
>
> They also spoke other false things (which out of modesty may not be written down) ...

The Primary Chronicle continued:

> Vladimir listened to them, for he was fond of women and indulgence, regarding which he heard with pleasure. But circumcision and abstinence from pork and wine were disagreeable to him. "Drinking," said he, "is the joy of the Russes. We cannot exist without that pleasure."

Next, Vladimir was visited by Germans from the Roman Catholic Church, and then from Jewish Khazars.

Finally Vladimir was visited by Greeks from the Eastern Orthodox Church, whose beautiful Hagia Sophia Cathedral in Constantinople was the largest and most ornate church in the world for over a thousand years. Russian messengers reported of it to Vladimir:

> We knew not whether we were in Heaven or on Earth ... We only know that God dwells there among the people, and their service is fairer than the ceremonies of other nations.

After hearing an explanation of the Gospel, and learning that the New Testament had been written in their language of Greek, and that many cities mentioned in the New Testament were located in the Byzantine Empire, Vladimir was baptized into Eastern Orthodox Christianity. He also adopted the Eastern Orthodox Saint Nicholas as the Patron Saint of Russia. There was, perhaps, not a city in Russia without a church named after Saint Nicholas.

Vladimir proceeded to have all Kievan Russians baptized into the Orthodox Christian Church. He sent his younger son, Yaroslav the Wise, to rule Novgorod.

Relations began to strain between Vladimir and his son, Yaroslav. When Vladimir died in 1015, his older son, Svyatopolk the Accursed, had three other brothers killed and seized power in Kiev.

The citizens of Novgorod supported Yaroslav

against Svyatopolk. Yaroslav finally won in 1019, and proceeded to reward the loyal citizens of Novgorod who supported him with privileges and freedoms. This effectively laid the foundation for an independent Novgorod Republic. Novgorod grew in wealth, constructed elaborate stone walls and erected the beautiful Church of Saint Sofia, the main cathedral of the Russian North.

By 1136, merchants had accumulated more power than the nobles, resulting in a government by the people. The neighboring city of Pskov, founded in 903, adhered politically to the Novgorod Republic. Novgorod and Pskov were the only major cities in Russia to escape destruction when the Mongols invaded in 1222, led by Batu Khan, the grandson of Genghis Khan.

In 1240, Novgorod invited Prince Alexander to protect it from the Swedish army. Alexander defeated the Swedes near the Neva River, resulting in his title – Alexander Nevsky. The main avenue in St. Petersburg is named for him: Nevski Prospekt.

In 1242, Alexander Nevsky saved Novgorod again from the nearby State of Teutonic Knights. He recaptured Pskov in a legendary campaign which included the Battle of the Ice on the frozen Lake Peipus, memorialized in Sergei Eisenstein's 1938 movie, *Alexander Nevsky.*

As the Mongols became their most powerful foe, Alexander Nevsky met in 1252 with the ruler of the Mongol "Golden Horde," Sartaq Khan, son of Batu Khan. Sartaq Khan had converted to Christianity.

Other Khan leaders became favorable to Christianity, including Hulagu Khan, another grandson of Genghis Khan, whose mother was a famous Christian princess – Sorghaghtani Beki. Hulagu Khan destroyed the Islamic capital of Baghdad (1258) and weakened Muslim control of Damascus (1260).

Hulagu Khan sent a letter in 1262 to French King Louis IX–St. Louis–proposing they fight together to recapture Jerusalem and drive Muslims out of Egypt:

> From the head of the Mongol army, anxious to devastate the perfidious nation of the Saracens (Muslims), with the good-will support of the Christian faith ... so that you, who are the rulers of the coasts on the other side of the sea, endeavor to deny a refuge for the Infidels, your enemies and ours, by having your subjects diligently patrol the seas.

Another grandson of Genghis Khan was Kublai Khan, Emperor of China, Korea, North India, Persia, Russia and Hungary. He had requested Marco Polo bring back 100 teachers of the Holy Christian Faith and a flask of oil from Christ's empty tomb in Jerusalem. Columbus referred to this in a letter to the King and Queen of Spain in 1492:

> Concerning the lands of India, and a Prince called Gran Khan ... How many times he sent to Rome to seek doctors in our Holy Faith to instruct him and that never had the Holy Father provided them, and thus so many people were lost through lapsing into idolatries ...

> And Your Highnesses ... devoted to the Holy Christian Faith ... enemies of the sect of Mahomet ... resolved to send me, Christopher Columbus, to the said regions of India, to see the said princes and peoples ... and the manner in which may be undertaken their conversion to our Holy Faith.

In Russia, Sartaq Khan granted Alexander Nevsky vassalage to become Grand Duke of Vladimir. In 1256, Sartaq Khan died mysteriously in what was suspected to have been poisoning by his uncle Berke Khan, who had converted to Islam.

Berke Khan took control of the Golden Horde and,

with his armies, spread Islam throughout the Mongolian Empire. Berke Khan declared war on Hulagu Khan for destroying the Islamic capital of Baghdad.

Muslim "Tartar" armies proceeded to capture most of the land of Rus, with the exception of Novgorod, as it was surrounded by swamps.

The Novgorod Republic continued to flourish, being ruled by its citizens. Elections were held in the city square. People gathered and shouted for their candidates. The candidate with the loudest supporters became ruler. Princes were still present in Novgorod, but only to be hired military leaders to protect the city.

Novgorod's fate began to change when Ivan III of Moscow, known as Ivan the Great, expanded his domain. In 1478, Ivan the Great took away four-fifths of the land from the Republic of Novgorod and deported its richest and ancient families.

A century later, in 1570, Ivan the IV, know as "the Terrible," became paranoid of conspiracies and killed anyone suspected of being disloyal, even his own son.

When the Novgorod Republic was rumored to be seeking an alliance with Poland-Lithuania, Ivan attacked with a vengeance. His first command was to subjugate the church. He stripped cathedrals and monasteries of their valuables; put priests and deacons in shackles and flogged them till they paid a ransom; and he ordered some 500 clergymen beaten to death.

Ivan laid waste to 90 percent of the farmland surrounding Novgorod. His 6,000 secret police, called Oprichniki, pillaged, burned, arrested and terrorized with cruel violence. Men, women and children were roasted over fires, tied to sleds and dragged through town, trapped under ice in the Volkhov River, and if they managed to surface, they were shoved back under.

According to *The First Pskov Chronicle*, an

estimated 60,000 people were senselessly slaughtered by Ivan the Terrible. Novgorod continued to decline until it finally lost its position of being the only Russian port near the Baltic when St. Petersburg was built.

∽

36. NEW FRANCE

In 1524, with war raging in Europe, the King of France, Francis I, sent Italian explorer Giovanni da Verrazzano to find a sea route to India and China.

Verrazzano sailed the coast of North American, being recognized as the first European to sail the area of Cape Fear, North Carolina, which he thought was the passage to China. He entered the mouth of the Hudson River and sailed along Long Island, up the coast to Cape Cod, Narragansett Bay, Nova Scotia and Newfoundland, before returning to France.

Verrazzano named the new land "Francesca," and his brother's map labeled it "Nova Gallia" or "New France," though the names did not go into common use.

A statue of Verrazzano stands in New York's Battery Park and on Rehoboth Beach in Delaware. Named for him are the Verrazano–Narrows Bridge across New York Harbor, the Jamestown Verrazzano Bridge, and Maryland's Verrazzano Bridge.

Verrazzano encountered inhabitants of the Lanape, Narragansett and Wampanoag tribes. On later voyages, he explored Brazil and the Bahamas. According to one account, he was killed and eaten by native Caribs on the island of Guadeloupe in 1528.

In 1534, France's King Francis I, sent explorer Jacques Cartier to sail west to find a sea route to Asia. Cartier described the land with the native Inuit word "Canada," which means "settlement."

In 1535, Francis I sent Cartier on a second voyage with the Commission (*Francis Parkman's Works,*

Volume 2, p. 38–39; Lescarbot, I. 411; Hazard, I. 19):

> We have resolved to send him again to the lands of Canada and Hochelaga (present-day Montreal), which form the extremity of Asia towards the west ... (with the object of the enterprise to be discovery, settlement, and conversion of) men without knowledge of God or use of reason.

Jacques Cartier sailed up the Saint Lawrence River till he came to impassable rapids near Montreal which he named "La Chine," meaning "The China" rapids, as he was convinced this was the Northwest Passage to Asia. An account of this expedition included the winter of 1535–1536 (*The Voyages of Jacques Cartier,* University of Toronto Press, 1993):

> Captain (Jacques Cartier) again asked them (natives) what was the trouble? They answered that their god, Cudouagny by name, had made an announcement at Hochelaga ... to tell them the tidings, which were that there would be so much ice and snow that all would perish.

> At this we all began to laugh and to tell them that their god Cudouagny was a mere fool who did not know what he was saying; and that they should tell their messengers as much; and that Jesus would keep them safe from the cold if they would trust in him.

> Thereupon Taignoagny and his companions asked the Captain if he had spoken with Jesus; and he replied that his priests had done so and that there would be fine weather.

That winter was extremely harsh, as described:

> Already several had died, whom for sheer weakness we had to bury beneath the snow; for ... the ground was frozen and we could not dig into it ...

> We were also in great dread of the people

of the country, lest they should become aware of our plight and helplessness. And to hide our sickness, our Captain, whom God kept continually in good health, whenever they came near the fort, would go out to meet them with two or three men ...

At this time so many men were down with this disease that we had almost lost hope of ever returning to France, when God in his infinite goodness and mercy had pity upon us and made known to us the most excellent remedy against all diseases that ever had been seen or heard of in the whole world.

In the account, Cartier learned of one who had:

... been healed by the juice of the leaves of a tree and the dregs of these, and that this was the only way to cure sickness. Upon this the Captain asked him if there was not some of it thereabouts ... They showed us how to grind the bark and the leaves and to boil the whole in water ... They called the tree in their language Annedda ...

In less than eight days, a whole tree as large and as tall as any I every saw was used up, and produced such a result that had all the doctors of Louvain and Montpellier been there with all the drugs of Alexandria, they could not have done so much in a year as did this tree in eight days; for it benefited us so much that all who were willing to use it recovered health and strength, thanks be to God.

Cartier gathered large amounts of gold and brought it back to France, only to find it was iron-pyrite – "fool's gold." He also seized Indian Chief Donnacona, his two sons and seven inhabitants and took them back to France, but nine of the ten died.

Writing of Jacques Cartier, the later French explorer Samuel de Champlain wrote in his *Voyages and*

Explorations (Volume I, Book I, Chapter II):

It is nothing new for the French to make sea voyages for conquest. We know very well that the discovery of new countries and noble enterprises on the sea were begun by our forefathers.

It was the Bretons and Normans who, in the year 1504, were the first Christians to discover the grand bank of the Codfish and the islands of the New World, as is noted in the histories of Niflet and of Antoine Maginus.

It is also very certain that in the time of King Francis I, in the year 1523, he sent Verazzano, a Florentine, to discover the lands, coasts and harbors of Florida, as the accounts of his voyages bear testimony; where, after having explored the coast from latitude 33 to latitude 47, just as he was thinking of making a home there, death put an end to his life and his plans.

After that, the same King Francis, persuaded by Messire Philip Chabot, Admiral of France, sent Jacques Cartier to discover new lands, and for this purpose he made two voyages in the years 1534 and 1535.

In the first he discovered the Island of Newfoundland and the Gulf of Saint Lawrence, with several other islands in this gulf, and he would have gone farther had not the severe season hastened his return.

This Jacques Cartier was from the city of St. Malo. He was thoroughly versed and experienced in seamanship; the equal of any one of his times. And St. Malo is under obligation to preserve his memory, for it was his greatest desire to discover new lands.

At the request of Charles de Mouy, Sieur de la Mailleres, at that time Vice-Admiral, he undertook the same voyage for the second time; and in order to compass his purpose and to have His Majesty lay the foundation of a colony to increase the honor of God and his royal authority, he gave his commissions with that of the aforesaid Sieur Admiral, who had the direction of this embarkation and contributed all he could to it.

When the commissions had been prepared, His Majesty put this same Cartier in charge, and he set sail with two vessels on May 16, 1535.

His voyage was so successful that he arrived at the Gulf of Saint Lawrence, entered the river with his ships of 800 tons burden, 6 and even got as far as an island a hundred and twenty leagues up the river, which he called the Isle of Orleans.

From there he went some ten leagues farther up the same stream to winter on a small river which is almost dry at low tide. This he named St. Croix, because he arrived there on the day of the Exaltation of the Holy Cross.

The place is now called the St. Charles River and at present the Recollect fathers and the Jesuit fathers are stationed there to found a seminary for the instruction of youth.

From there Cartier went up the river some sixty leagues, as far as a place which was called Ochelaga in his time and is now called Grand Sault St. Louis.

It was inhabited by savages who were sedentary and cultivated the soil. This they no longer do, because of the wars that have made them withdraw into the interior.

In 1541, Cartier embarked on his third and final expedition, but was rebuffed by the native inhabitants. At the same time, Frances I sent Sieur Jean-Francois de Roberval on an expedition.

Roberval had a career raiding Spanish ships in the Caribbean, similar to England's Sir Francis Drake and Sir Walter Raleigh. Francis I gave Roberval a commission and a title, first Lieutenant General of New France (*Lettres Patentes accorde'es a' Jehan Francoys de la Rogue Sr de Roberval*, January 15, 1541):

> Francis, by the grace of God, King of France, to all to whom these presents may come, greetings. Since desiring to hear and learn about several countries ...

> Whereas we have undertaken this voyage for the honor of God our Creator, desiring with all our hearts to do that which shall be agreeable to Him, it is our will to perform a compassionate and meritorious work towards criminals and malefactors, to the end that they may acknowledge the Creator, return thanks to Him, and mend their lives.

> Therefore we have resolved to cause to be delivered to our aforesaid lieutenant (Sieur de Roberval) such and so many of the aforesaid criminals and malefactors detained in our prisons as may seem to him useful and necessary to be carried to the aforesaid countries.

A harsh leader, Roberval named his settlement Charlesbourg-Royal in 1541, near present-day Quebec.

After two years, the settlement was abandoned. Roberval and the colonists returned to France. He soon resumed pirating Spanish ships in the Caribbean. Roberval died in 1560, being considered one of the first Protestant Huguenot victims in the Wars of Religion.

Francis I persecuted religious dissidents, killing thousands in the Massacre of the Waldensians of Mérindol in 1545. When Francis I died in 1547, his son, Henry II became king.

37. LIST OF FRENCH MONARCHS

At this point, it would be helpful to see a list of French monarchs during this era.

The House of Valois:

- •Francis I, reigned 1515–1547;
- •Henry II, reigned 1547–1559, with his wife was Catherine de' Medici;
- •Francis II, reigned 1559–1560, with his mother Catherine de' Medici;
- •Charles IX, reigned 1560–1574, with his mother Catherine de' Medici;
- •Henry III, reigned 1574–1589, with his mother Catherine de' Medici.

The House of Bourbon:

- •Good King Henry IV of Navarre, reigned 1589–1610, till he was assassinated;
- •Louis XIII, reigned 1610–1643;
- •Louis XIV–The Sun King, reigned 1643–1715;

✑

38. CATHERINE DE MEDICI

France's King Henry II married Catherine de' Medici, the daughter of Lorenzo de' Medici, to whom Niccolò Machiavelli dedicated his notorious book, *The Prince*, 1515. Catherine was the niece of Pope Clement VII, who refused to recognize Henry VIII's divorce.

In 1559, Henry II died. His son Francis II became king of France, ruling with direction from his mother.

Francis II was only 14-years-old when he married the 16-year-old Mary–Queen of Scots in 1558. The popular fictionalized TV series *Reign* (CW) features the character Mary–Queen of Scots.

France wanted Scotland to stay Catholic and independent of Protestant England. When young King

Francis II died in 1560 at age 16, Mary–Queen of Scots, now age 18, was returned to Scotland in 1561, where she was confronted by Reformer John Knox.

Francis II's mother, Catherine de' Medici, then assumed the role of regent, ruling France on behalf of her next son, the ten-year-old son Charles IX. Religious persecutions continued with tragedies such as the Massacre of Wassy in 1562.

ᕤ

39. SPANISH DRIVE FRENCH FROM FLORIDA

In 1562, some Protestant Huguenots fled France's persecutions, led by Jean Ribault and René Goulaine de Laudonnière. They attempted to settle in an area of the New World called Florida.

Ribault founded a French outpost called Charlesfort on Parris Island, near the place where the Spanish had attempted the settlement of San Miguel de Gualdape in 1526. This was abandoned and in 1564, the French settled on the banks of Florida's St. John's River.

Spain considered these settlements as encroachments into their territory, as Spain had claimed all the New World since the time of Columbus' voyage of 1492. The area of the Caribbean Sea controlled by Spain was called the "Spanish Main."

In 1565, Spain put an end to the French Huguenot settlement of Fort Caroline, Florida. Congressman Charles E. Bennett commemorated them by sponsoring a bill, September 21, 1950, to establish Fort Caroline National Memorial. In 1989, Rep. Bennett recited:

> The 425th anniversary of the beginning settlements by Europeans ... renamed from Fort Caroline to San Mateo, to San Nicolas, to Cowford and finally to Jacksonville in 1822 ... Three small ships carrying 300 Frenchmen led by Rene de Laudonniere anchored in the river known today as the St. Johns ...

> On June 30, 1564, construction of a triangular–shaped fort ... was begun with the help of a local tribe of Timucuan Indians ... Home for this hardy group of Huguenots ... their strong religious ... motivations inspired them.

The French Christian Huguenots in Florida set a day of Thanksgiving and offered the first Protestant prayer in North America on June 30, 1564:

> We sang a psalm of Thanksgiving unto God, beseeching Him that it would please Him to continue His accustomed goodness towards us.

Bennett related the colony's unfortunate end:

> Fort Caroline existed but for a short time ... Spain ... captured ... the fort and ... slaughtered most of its inhabitants in September of 1565.

After massacring the French at Fort Caroline, the Spanish Governor of Florida, Don Pedro Menéndez de Avilés, founded St. Augustine in 1565 – the first *permanent* European settlement in North America.

~~

40. ST. BARTHOLOMEW'S DAY MASSACRE

Back in France, in 1572, Catherine de' Medici arranged for her daughter, Margaret, to marry Henry of Navarre, who had been baptized Catholic, but was raised as a Protestant Huguenot.

He was in the royal line, being a descendant of French King Louis IX – Saint Louis – who led the 7th and 8th crusades against the Muslims.

Henry of Navarre and Margaret's wedding took place in Paris on August 18, 1572.

With so many Protestant aristocrats and leaders in Paris for the wedding, Catherine de' Medici is credited with arranging the St. Bartholomew's Day Massacre just a few days afterwards, August 23, 1572.

An estimated 30,000 Huguenot Protestants were

killed and the Seine River was choked with floating bodies. Henry of Navarre barely escaped from Paris.

Many Protestant Huguenots fled France during the French Wars of Religion, which raged on and off from 1562 to 1598, resulting in the deaths of approximately three million from battles, famine, and disease.

This was Europe's deadliest period of religious wars until the Thirty Years' War, 1618–1648, which took place in the German kingdoms, resulting in eight million deaths.

Young Charles IX died in 1574, and Catherine de' Medici's next son became King Henry III.

Henry III's younger brother, the Duke of Anjou, joined Protestants in laying siege to Paris. To call off the siege, Henry III issued the Edict of Beaulieu of 1576, granting Protestant Huguenots freedom of worship. Later that year, after threats of the siege passed, Henry III disregarded the Edict and resumed persecutions.

Henry III appointed France's first Consul to the court of Morocco's prince Abd al-Malik. When Henry III was assassinated in 1589, it left Henry of Navarre as next in line to be King of France.

Known as Henry IV or "Good King Henry of Navarre," he brought a temporary halt to the French Wars of Religion by issuing the Edict of Nantes in 1598, which granted toleration to Huguenots.

৵

41. SAMUEL DE CHAMPLAIN

In 1603, Good King Henry of Navarre sent Samuel de Champlain to settle New France (Canada).

In 1605, Champlain, considered "the Father of New France," together with Pierre Du Gua de Monts, founded Port Royal as the first capital of French Acadia.

In 1608, Champlain founded Quebec City near the Indian settlement of "Stadacona."

In 1609, he encountered the lake which was named for him – Lake Champlain – draining north into the Saint Lawrence River Valley of Canada.

Champlain's travels are documented in *The Voyages and Explorations of Samuel de Champlain (1604-1616)*, translated by Annie Nettleton Bourne, and in *Voyage of 1603*, reprinted from *Purchas His Pilgrimes*, edited by Yale History Professor Edward Gaylod Bourne, with an introduction by W.L. Grant, M.A., who stated:

> The history of Western Civilization begins in a conflict with the Orient, a conflict of which it maybe the end is not yet. But the routes between East and West have been trodden by the caravans of trade more often even than by the feet of armies.
>
> The treasures of the East were long brought overland to Alexandria, or Constantinople, or the cities of the Levant, and thence distributed to Europe by the galleys of Genoa or of Venice.
>
> But when the Turk placed himself astride the Bosporus, and made Egypt his feudatory, new routes had to be found.
>
> In the search for these were made the three greatest voyages in history, those of Columbus, of Vasco da Gama, and greatest of all of Magellan.
>
> In his search for the riches of Cipangu, Columbus stumbled upon America.
>
> The great Genoese lived and died under the illusion that he had reached the outmost verge of Asia; and though even in his lifetime men realized that what he had found was no less than a new world. America was long looked on as an unwelcome obstacle of unknown extent across the path of the Eastern trader.

Farther and farther men ranged the coast, seeking into every bay and estuary, in the vain hope that the South Sea might open to their gaze. To southwards, Magellan found a strait, but the journey was long and dangerous, and open only to the ships of Spain.

To northwards France took up the search, and it was in quest of the Orient that Jacques Cartier put out from St. Malo.

For a moment Chaleur Bay seemed to him the strait of his dream, but soon he came to its end, "whereof we were much torn with grief," he says in his quaint old French.

On his next voyage he went in vain up the St. Lawrence as far as Montreal; but the terrors of a Canadian winter, with its attendant scurvy, and the still greater horrors of the Wars of Religion, for the next half-century restricted the French to fishing voyages to Newfoundland and the Gulf of St. Lawrence.

With the Peace of Vervins and the Edict of Nantes in 1598, France had rest from foreign and civil strife, and turned again to the nobler task of exploration.

This was the quest to which the sea-captain of Brouage, Samuel de Champlain, gave the best years of his life, "always traveling–with an hungry heart," with the great South Sea ever a day's journey in advance.

Tired at last, he gave himself up to establish on the rock of Quebec a station from which his successors might fare forth.

In his search for the South Sea he had been the first great explorer of Canada, and this series of "Trail Makers of the North" appropriately begins with his undaunted name.

As the new world opened out, the search for the Orient took a second place.

Even in the days of Champlain, his partners thought chiefly of trade with the natives, and in the next two centuries a series of great fur-trading companies, English and French, took toll of the country, and pushed ever farther west and north ...

Canada had entered upon the experiment of seeking to make in the West a great civilization from the off-scourings of Europe.

Samuel de Champlain wrote in Volume I, Book I, Chapter II, of his *Voyages and Explorations*:

That Kings and great Princes ought to take more pains to spread the knowledge of the true God and magnify His glory among barbarians than to multiply their states.

The most illustrious palms and laurels that kings and princes can win in this world are contempt for temporal blessings and the desire to gain the spiritual.

They cannot do this more profitably than by converting, through their labor and piety, to the catholic, apostolic and Roman religion, an infinite number of savages, who live without faith, without law, with no knowledge of the true God.

For the taking of forts, the winning of battles, and the conquests of countries, are nothing in comparison with the reward of those who prepare for themselves crowns in heaven, unless it be fighting against infidels. In that case, war is not only necessary, but just and holy, since the safety of Christianity, the glory of God and the defense of the faith are at stake.

These labors are, in themselves, praiseworthy and very commendable, besides being in conformity to the commandment of God, which says, That the conversion of an infidel is of more value than the conquest of a kingdom.

And if all this cannot move us to seek after heavenly blessings at least as passionately as after those of the earth, it is because men's covetousness for this world's blessings is so great that most of them do not care for the conversion of infidels so long as their fortune corresponds to their desires, and everything conforms to their wishes.

Moreover, it is this covetousness that has ruined and is wholly ruining the progress and advancement of this enterprise, which is not yet well under way, and is in danger of collapsing, unless His Majesty establishes there conditions as righteous, charitable and just as he is himself;

and unless he himself takes pleasure in learning what can be done to increase the glory of God and to benefit his state, repelling the envy of those who should support this enterprise, but who seek its ruin rather than its success.

❧

42. SCOTLAND

Back in 1560, after France's 16-year-old King Francis II died, his young widow, Mary–Queen of Scots, at age 18, returned to Scotland. Upon arrival in 1561, she was immediately criticized from the pulpit by Protestant Reformer John Knox.

Earlier in his career, in 1547, at the age of 34, John Knox was arrested sentenced to be a galley slave on a French ship. Sailing away from Scotland, John Knox looked up as they passed St. Andrews and said:

I see the steeple of that place where God first in public opened my mouth to glory; and I am fully persuaded ... I shall not depart this life till my tongue shall glorify his godly name in the same place.

After two years, John Knox was released and exiled to England. He rose to be the royal chaplain to England's young Protestant King Edward VI. Knox influenced Thomas Crammer, Archbishop of Canterbury, in his compiling of the Church of England's Book of Common Prayer.

When King Edward VI died in 1553, his sister Mary I, "Bloody Mary," took the throne and attempted to bring England back under the Catholic Church.

In 1554, John Knox escaped England to Geneva, Switzerland, where he met Protestant Reformer John Calvin. Through Knox, Calvin's beliefs influenced Scotland and the millions of Scots, Scots–Irish, Puritan and Presbyterian immigrants who came to America.

The influence of John Calvin was noted in *TIME Magazine's* article "Looking to Its Roots" (May 25, 1987):

> Ours is the only country deliberately founded on a good idea.

> That good idea combines a commitment to man's inalienable rights with the Calvinist belief in an ultimate moral right and sinful man's obligation to do good.

> These articles of faith, embodied in the Declaration of Independence and in the Constitution, literally govern our lives today.

Secretary of the Navy George Bancroft published a ten–volume *History of the United States,* the first comprehensive history of America, in which he wrote:

> He who will not honor the memory and respect the influence of Calvin knows little of the origin of American liberty.

Calvin advised Jeanne d'Albret Queen Regnant of Navarre:

> Now that the government is in your hands, God will test your zeal and fidelity. You

now have an obligation to purge your lands of idolatry by taking into consideration the difficulties which can hold you back, the fears and doubts which can sap courage.

And I do not doubt that your advisors, if they look to this world, will try to stop you. I know the arguments advanced to prove that princes should not force their subjects to lead a Christian life, but all kingdoms which do not serve that of Jesus Christ are ruined. So judge for yourself. I do not say that all can be done in a day.

Calvin told Queen Regnant of Navarre, April 28, 1545:

A dog barks when his master is attacked. I would be a coward if I saw that God's truth is attacked and yet would remain silent.

In 1559, John Knox returned to Scotland and followed Calvin's example of confronting monarchs. He stated: "A man with God is always in the majority."

Knox preached a sermon in St. Andrews Cathedral which incited hearers to smash statues and loot Catholic churches. Through his efforts, the Scottish Parliament officially accepted the Reformation in 1560, beginning the Presbyterian Church.

Knox publicly confronted Mary–Queen of Scots, who had a tragic personal life. After returning from France, she had married Lord Darnley in 1565, but he became jealous of Mary's private secretary, David Rizzio, and had him murdered.

Lord Darnley was then suspiciously killed two years later in an explosion. The chief suspect in his murder was the Earl of Bothwell, who manipulated Mary into marrying him a month later. This upheaval resulted in the Scottish Parliament forcing Mary to abdicate her throne. She was replaced by her and Lord Darnley's infant son, James.

In 1567, at the age of 13 months, James was crowned King James VI of Scotland. John Knox gave the coronation sermon.

The Earl of Bothwell tried to raise forces to return Mary–Queen of Scots to her throne, but he was captured in Norway and died in prison.

Mary–Queen of Scots fled to England in 1568 to be protected by her cousin, Queen Elizabeth I, the daughter of Henry VIII and Anne Boleyn. Elizabeth turned this protection into a forced custody for 19 years.

∽

43. EDWARD VI

When Henry VIII died in 1547, his son by Jane Seymour was crowned King Edward VI. He was 9-years-old. In 1551, Edward enlisted Sebastian Cabot, son of Italian explorer John Cabot, to find a passage to China.

Being one of the first ever "companies," the Company of Merchant Adventurers to New Lands was incorporated in 1553. The three ship expedition intended to sail to Cathay (China) and the Moluccas Spice Islands. They made a tragic mistake by sailing from England, northeast over Russia.

Separated in a storm in the North Sea, two of the ships were frozen in ice, resulting in everyone on board freezing to death. The third ship, commanded by Richard Chancellor, made it as far as the White Sea and the mouth of the Dvina River.

Russians took Richard Chancellor to Moscow where he was received by Tsar Ivan the Terrible. Chancellor returned to England in 1554 with a letter from the Tsar welcoming trade. The company was rechartered under Mary I in 1555 as the Muscovy Company, with Sebastian Cabot as its governor.

The company not only sent envoys to Russia, but

sent them to travel south of Russia to the Safavid Persian Empire. This began numerous trading visits of English merchants, Robert Sherley and Anthony Sherley with Shah Abbas I at his new capital of Isfahan.

⚜

44. "BLOODY" MARY

Edward VI reigned 6 years and died at the age of 15, on July 6, 1553. He had chosen as his successor his first cousin once removed, Lady Jane Grey, but she was ousted after only 9 days by supporters of Mary I, the daughter of Henry VIII by Catherine of Aragon.

Mary I married Philip II of Spain, son of Charles V. Philip had inherited the global Spanish empire, with the Philippine Islands being named for him.

Mary I ruled England for only 5 years. During her brief reign, her government executed Lady Jane Grey – the Nine Day Queen, as well as 300 others, resulting in her nickname "Bloody Mary."

She burned at the stake the Oxford Martyrs: Bishop Hugh Latimer, who had been Edward VI's chaplain; Rev. Nicholas Ridley, who had been the Bishop of London; and Thomas Crammer, the former Archbishop of the Anglican Church.

Facing execution, October 16, 1555, Bishop Hugh Latimer exhorted Bishop Nicholas Ridley:

> Play the man, Master Ridley. We shall this day light such a candle, by God's grace, in England, as I trust shall never be put out.

When Mary died on November 17, 1558, her half-sister Elizabeth I became Queen.

⚜

45. LIST OF ENGLISH MONARCHS

At this point, it may be helpful to see the list of England's monarchs during this era:

The House of Tudor:
- •Henry VII, reigned 1485–1509;
- •Henry VIII, reigned 1509–1547, six wives;
- •Edward VI, reigned 1547–1553, died at age 15;
- •Lady Jane Grey, reigned nine days from July 10–19, 1553;
- •Mary I, reigned 1553–1558, married Spain's Philip II;
- •Elizabeth I, reigned 1558–1603, called the Virgin Queen as she never married.

The House of Stuart:
- •James I, reigned 1603–1625; namesake of Jamestown and the King James Bible.
- •Charles I, reigned 1625–1649, beheaded;

The English Commonwealth:
- •Rump Parliament, 1649–1653;
- •Oliver Cromwell, reigned 1653–1658;
- •Richard Cromwell, reigned 1658–1659.

The restored House of Stuart:
- •Charles II, reigned, 1660–1685;
- •James II, Duke of York, reigned 1685–1688, exiled;
- •Mary II and William III–the Dutch Prince of Orange, co-reigned 1688–1702;
- •Anne, reigned, 1702–1714.

46. ELIZABETHAN ERA

Elizabeth I was born September 7, 1533, the daughter of Henry VIII by Anne Boleyn. Balancing religious views with political practicality, Elizabeth replied at her Coronation in 1558, when questioned as to the presence of Christ in the Sacrament:

Christ was the Word that spake it,

He took the bread and brake it,

And what that Word did make it,

I do believe and take it.

Elizabeth stated:

There is only one Christ, Jesus, one faith.
All else is a dispute over trifles.

She told William Lambarde in 1601:

He that will forget God, will also forget his
benefactors.

Elizabeth, the last Tudor monarch, stated in 1566:

I am your Queen. I will never be by violence
constrained to do anything. I thank God I am
endued with such qualities that if I were turned
out of the Realm in my petticoat I were able to
live in any place in Christendom.

She told the House of Commons in The Golden
Speech, November 30, 1601:

Though God hath raised me high, yet this
I count the glory of my Crown, that I have
reigned with your loves ... I do not so much
rejoice that God hath made me to be a Queen,
as to be a Queen over so thankful a people ...

The title of a King is a glorious title, but ...
we well know ... that we also are to yield an
account of our actions before the Great Judge.

Responding to questions from Parliament regarding
succession after her death, Elizabeth stated:

I know I am but mortal and so therewhilst
prepare myself for death, whensoever it shall
please God to send it.

In 1570, Pope Pius V excommunicated Queen
Elizabeth I. Regarding her epitaph, Elizabeth I said:

I am no lover of pompous title, but only
desire that my name may be recorded in a
line or two, which shall express my name,
my virginity, the years of my reign, and the
reformation of religion under it.

Elizabeth continued the Anglican Church begun when her father separated from Rome. A group that wanted to "purify" the Anglican Church were called "Puritans," who wanted to separate even more from Rome.

Another group gave up trying to purify the Anglican Church and decided to separate themselves–being called "separatists" or "Pilgrims." They eventually fled to Holland, and later to America.

During the 45 year reign of Queen Elizabeth I, the scientific revolution was begun by Sir Francis Bacon (1561–1626). In his treatise titled, *Of Atheism*, Sir Francis Bacon declared:

> A little philosophy inclineth man's mind to atheism, but depth in philosophy bringeth men's minds about to religion.

A contemporary of Francis Bacon was Italian astronomer Galileo Galilei (1564–1642), who made the first practical use of the telescope. Galileo stated:

> I am inclined to think that the authority of Holy Scripture is intended to convince men of those truths which are necessary for their salvation, which, being far above man's understanding, can not be made credible by any learning, or any other means than revelation by the Holy Spirit.

Galileo's work gave credence to the heliocentric theory of Polish astronomer Nicolaus Copernicus (1473–1543), where the sun is the center of the solar system, replacing Ptolemy's geocentric theory of the earth being the center.

Copernicus' heliocentric theory was advanced by Johannes Kepler (1571–1630). Kepler discovered the laws governing planetary motion and pioneered the discipline of celestial mechanics, known as Kepler's Laws, which aided Sir Isaac Newton (1642–1726) in his formulation of the theory of gravitation.

Kepler wrote in *The Harmonies of the World*, 1619:

> O, Almighty God, I am thinking Thy thoughts after Thee!

During Queen Elizabeth's reign, William Shakespeare wrote plays. Born on April 23, 1564, he died the same day in 1616.

Shakespeare wrote 38 plays which impacted world literature. He married Ann Hathaway, had three children, moved to London, and became shareholding director of Globe Theater.

His classics include: *Hamlet; Macbeth; Othello; King Lear;* and *A Midsummer Night's Dream.*

In 1609, the English ship *Sea Venture*, under Captain Christopher Newport, was sailing on the third supply mission to the Colony of Jamestown. It was caught in a hurricane and shipwrecked on the island of Bermuda for nine months.

An Englishman who was on the *Sea Venture* was Richard Rich. He recounted the voyage to Virginia in a narrative poem of twenty-two eight-line verses, titled, *Newes from Virginia: The Lost Flock Triumphant,* published in London, October 1, 1610, by Edw. Allde.

The poem contained the account of their shipwreck on the "Bermoothawes" (Bermudas), stating:

> With the happy Arrivall of that famous and worthy Knight Sr. Thomas Gates: and the well-reputed and valiant Captaine Mr Christopher Newport, and others, into England. With the maner of their distresse in the Hand of Devils (otherwise called Bermoothawes), where they remayned 42 weeks, and builded two Pynaces, in which they returned into Virginia. By R. Rich, Gent., one of the Voyage (1610).

Richard Rich wrote:

> God will not let us fall ... For ... our work is

good; We hope to plant a nation, Where none before hath stood.

Following Richard Rich's publishing his account of the *Sea Venture* being shipwrecked in a hurricane, Shakespeare wrote his play *The Tempest* (1610–1611).

In 1579, the Oxford educated priest Thomas Stephens, was one of the first western Christian missionaries, and probably the first Englishman, to reach India. He helped convert many of the upper Indian society, writing *Kristpurana–The Story of Christ.* He died in India in 1619.

In 1599, John Mildenhall and Richard Newman set off to become some of the first Englishmen to reach India by traveling over land. Acting as a representative for the British East India Company, John Mildenhall died there in 1614, considered to be the first Englishman buried in India.

In 1600, English navigator William Adams, sailing for the Dutch East India Company, arrived in Japan. He spent the next 10 years advising the shogun (military dictator) Tokugawa Ieyasu.

๛

47. EL DRAQUE

Sir Francis Drake was born around 1540 amid religious upheaval in England. During the Prayer Book Rebellion in 1549, his poor farmer father, Edward Drake, fled with his family to the coast where they lived on an old laid-up ship.

Edward Drake was ordained as a Protestant minister and preached to sailors in the King's Navy, afterwards becoming a vicar of Upchurch on the Medway.

Around the age of 12, Francis Drake was apprenticed to a ship transporting merchandise from France. The ship's master, having no children, eventually bequeathed the ship to Francis, which began his prosperous sailing career.

Drake held religious services on his ship twice a day. He sailed numerous times to the Caribbean for trade, and while there, he raided Spanish ships and settlements. His raids were so devastating, that King Philip II of Spain called him a pirate, El Draque, and offering the equivalent of six million dollars for his life.

In 1577, Sir Francis Drake began the second voyage in history to circumnavigate the globe. This was almost 60 years after Ferdinand Magellan's first voyage.

Drake sailed down the coast of South America and before Tierra del Fuego, passed through the Strait of Magellan. Through violent storms, he sailed and raided the Pacific Spanish coast of America north to California. At Mocha Island, hostile Mapuche attacked Drake, seriously injuring him with an arrow.

In 1579, Drake anchored north of San Francisco at "Drake's Bay." In the name of the Holy Trinity, he claimed California for the English Crown, calling it Nova Albion, which is Latin for "New Britain."

Turning west, Drake his ship, *Golden Hind,* sailed to the Spice Moluccas Islands of Indonesia, where he almost sank on a reef. Drake made it across the Indian Ocean, around Cape of Good Hope and up the coast of Africa back to England in 1580, where he was knighted by Queen Elizabeth I.

In 1588, Drake helped repel the Spanish Armada from invading England. He died aboard the ship, *Defiance,* January 28, 1596, after a failed attempt to capture San Juan, Puerto Rico.

President Ronald Reagan stated in his address after the *Challenger* explosion, January 28, 1986:

> There's a coincidence today. On this day 390 years ago, the great explorer Sir Francis Drake died aboard ship off the coast of Panama.

In his lifetime the great frontiers were the oceans, and a historian later said, "He lived by the sea, died on it, and was buried in it."

Well, today we can say of the *Challenger* crew: Their dedication was, like Drake's, complete.

✌

48. SPANISH FURIES

One of Spain's most famous commanders was the Duke of Alba, known as the "Iron Duke." Under Charles V, he fought in the Ottoman–Habsburg Wars, and captured Tunis, North Africa, in 1535.

In 1571, Spain successfully stopped the Ottoman fleet at the Battle of Lepanto, but declined to free the rest of the Mediterranean from Muslim control. Instead, it turned its attention to stop the Reformation from spreading in the Netherlands, Belgium, Burgundy, Luxembourg, and England.

Beginning in 1572, the Iron Duke was sent crush the Reformation in Holland. His men pillaged, burned, raped and slaughtered from 1572 to 1576 in what was called the "Spanish Furies." This was at the beginning of Holland's "Eighty Years' War" for independence.

With his "show no mercy" orders, the Iron Duke sacked and decimated the rebellious Dutch cities of Diest, Roermond, Guelders, Mons, Mechelen, Zutphen, Haarlem, Alkmaar. In the city of Naarden, every man, woman and child was massacred.

Dutch citizens of Leiden knew if they surrendered they would be killed as an example for others not to rebel. Half of the city's population died of starvation.

With their will bolstered to resist, William the Silent–Prince of Orange, with help from Elizabeth I, broke the dikes allowing sea water to flood the Spanish troops. He then sent rescuers on flat boats to bring herring and white bread to the starving citizens.

Finally, in 1574, Spain siege of Leiden was broken. To celebrate, William of Orange founded Leiden University, and citizens held an annual Day of Thanks giving. Since the Pilgrims moved to Leiden in 1609, they would have experienced the city's annual fall thanksgiving commemorating the lifting of Spain's siege.

Dutch historian Jeremy Dupertuis Bangs (Ph.D. Leiden, 1976), in "1621: A Historian Looks Anew at Thanksgiving," considered what influenced the Pilgrims' thanksgiving, noting that William Brewster's friend, Jan Orlers, wrote of Leiden's Thanksgiving:

> Every year throughout the city a General Day of Prayer and Thanksgiving ... held and celebrated on the Third of October, to thank and praise God Almighty that he so mercifully had saved the city from her enemies.

In 1579, seven former Spanish provinces united with the Union of Utrecht, which is considered the foundation of the Republic of the Seven United Provinces.

Finally, in 1648, after 80 years of war, Spain was forced to recognize the independence of the Dutch Republic with the Peace of Westphalia. Beginning as a republic, Holland's government eventually took the form of a limited constitutional monarchy.

❧

49. LIST OF DUTCH STADTHOLDERS

Dutch heads of state, called "stadtholders," of the House of Orange-Nassau, were:

- William the Silent, Prince of Orange, in office 1544–1584, led Dutch revolt against Spain;
- Philip William, Prince of Orange, but captive in Spain;
- Maurice, Prince of Orange, 1585–1625;
- Frederick Henry, Prince of Orange, 1625–1647;
- William II, Prince of Orange, 1647–1650,

married Mary, the daughter of England's King Charles I. His brother-in-law was England's King Charles II.

•William III, Prince of Orange, 1650–1702, married Mary, daughter of England's King James II. In the Glorious Revolution of 1688, William and Mary ruled England as co-regents. When Mary died in 1694, William III became King, though the House of Commons required him to accepted an English Bill of Rights.

❧

50. RALEIGH'S LOST COLONY

Sir Walter Raleigh (1554–1618) was the cousin of Sir Richard Grenville, renown English naval commander who fought the Spanish. Raleigh was also the younger half-brother of Sir Humphrey Gilbert, renown English soldier and early colonizer.

In 1584, Raleigh received a Charter to began a colony in America, which he named "Virginia," after the "Virgin Queen Elizabeth I." The Charter stated:

Elizabeth, by the Grace of God of England ... Defender of the Faith ... grant to our trusty and well beloved servant Walter Raleigh ... to discover ... barbarous lands ... not actually possessed of any Christian Prince, nor inhabited by Christian People ...

Upon ... finding ... such remote lands ... it shall be necessary for the safety of all men ... to live together in Christian peace ... Ordinances ... agreeable to ... the laws ... of England, and also so as they be not against the true Christian faith.

In 1585, Sir Walter Raleigh established the settlement at Roanoke Island, in present-day North Carolina. Unfortunately, during the crisis of the Spanish Armada attacking England in 1588, the Roanoke Colony was ignored for three years, leaving the settlers on their own.

When supply ships finally returned to Roanoke in 1590, they found the settlement abandoned, resulting in it being referred to as "The Lost Colony."

Raleigh suffered a major financial loss, 40 thousand pounds, in his attempt to found the Roanoke colony,

∽

51. SPANISH ARMADA

In 1554, Spain's Philip II married England's Mary I–"Bloody Mary," making him technically a co-ruler of England. When Mary died suddenly in 1558, Elizabeth took England's throne, but Philip II felt the English throne belonged to him. Philip proposed to marry Elizabeth, but she declined.

An undercurrent spread that if Philip could marry Mary–Queen of Scots, he could lay claim to the English throne. When rumors arose in England of a possible plot to assassinate her, Elizabeth executed dozens, including, sadly, her first cousin once removed, Mary–Queen of Scots, in 1587.

Elizabeth's fears of being assassinated were not unfounded. During this time in France, there were numerous attempts to assassinate Good King Henry of Navarre.

At this time in Elizabeth's reign, Catholics went into hiding or fled. Priests sent to England were captured and executed.

On May 19, 1588, King Philip II of Spain, who was the most powerful leader in the world at the time, sent his invincible Spanish Armada to invade England.

Spain's threat to England had been so great that Queen Elizabeth felt the need to make a treaty with Spain's enemies, the Ottoman Sultan Murad III and the Moroccan ruler Mulai Ahmad al-Mansur.

The Spanish Armada consisted of 130 ships, with

1,500 brass guns and 1,000 iron guns, carrying 8,000 sailors and 18,000 soldiers.

They were planning on picking up another 30,000 more soldiers from the Spanish Netherlands. Spain's Dunkirk Privateers raided English and Dutch ships.

Queen Elizabeth put on her armor and rallied England with her most famous speech, August 9, 1588:

> Let tyrants fear, I have always so behaved myself, that under God I have placed my chiefest strength and safeguard in the loyal hearts and goodwill of my subjects ...

> I am come amongst you ... resolved, in the midst and heat of battle, to live or die amongst you all – to lay down for my God, and for my kingdoms, and for my people, my honor and my blood even in the dust ...

Elizabeth continued:

> I know I have the body of a weak and feeble woman; but I have the heart and stomach of a king – and of a King of England too, and think foul scorn that Parma or Spain, or any prince of Europe, should dare to invade the borders of my realm ...

> I myself will take up arms, I myself will be your general ... By your valor in the field, we shall shortly have a famous victory over those enemies of my God, of my kingdom, and of my people.

Queen Elizabeth relied on Sir Francis Drake, Sir John Hawkins, Sir Martin Frobisher and Lord Howard of Effingham, whose smaller vessels were faster and more maneuverable vessels were able to elude the enormous Spanish galleons which attacked at port of Plymouth, England.

After Spain's initial attacks, the English counter–attacked. Sir Francis Drake's smaller, more maneuverable vessels proved difficult to catch.

The Spanish Armada regrouped on the other side of the English Channel near the French port of Calais.

The fast flyboats of Dutch Admiral Justinus van Nassau captured two Spanish galleons, whose deep–drafts put them at a disadvantage in shallow waters.

With weather getting tempestuous and with no deep water port, the Spanish Armada anchored off the coast in a tightly–packed defensive crescent formation.

At midnight, July 28, 1588, Sir Francis Drake positioned 8 ships upwind of the Spanish fleet, set them on fire and let them drift downwind toward the anchored Spanish Armada.

In a panic, Spanish ships cut their anchor cables and drifted apart. The next morning, July 29, 1588, the English attacked in the Battle of Gravelines. Hurricane–force winds and dangerous currents arose scattering the Spanish Armada and carrying the sea battle north toward Scotland.

As the Armada was blown along the northern coast of Scotland and down the western coast of Ireland, gale force winds dashed the ships against the rocks. The Spanish Armada suffered 56 ships wrecked, sunk or captured, 10 ships scuttled, and over 20,000 dead from battle, storms and disease.

When King Philip II of Spain learned of the loss, he exclaimed:

> I sent the Armada against men, not God's winds and waves.

As a result of these losses, Spain suffered several bankruptcies. A coin minted in Holland in 1588 had engraved on one side Spanish ships sinking and on the other side men kneeling under the inscription "Man Proposeth, God Disposeth."

Had Spain won, there would have been no Anglican England, no Puritans, no Pilgrims, no New England and no United States. North America would have remained been an extension of New Spain–Mexico.

Woodrow Wilson wrote of the Spanish Armada in *History of the American People* (1902, Vol. 1, Ch 1):

> For England the end of Spain's power was marked by the destruction of the Armada, and the consequent dashing of all the ambitious schemes that had been put aboard the imposing fleet at Lisbon ...

> The great Armada came ... Spain recognized in the smartly handled craft which beat her clumsy galleons up the Channel the power that would some day drive her from the seas. Her hopes went to pieces with that proud fleet, before English skill and prowess and pitiless sea–weather.

Describing English ships, Theodore Roosevelt and Henry Cabot Lodge wrote in *Hero Tales From American History* (1895):

> The ships ... which ... won glory in the War of 1812 were essentially like those with which Drake and Hawkins and Frobisher had harried the Spanish armadas two centuries and a half earlier. They were wooden sailing–vessels, carrying many guns mounted in broadside.

Woodrow Wilson gave background details:

> Henry VIII interested himself in improved methods of ship–building; and when he had time to think of it he encouraged instruction in seamanship and navigation; but he built no navy.

> He even left the English coasts without adequate police, and suffered his subjects to defend themselves as best they might against the pirates who infested the seas not only, but came once and again to cut vessels out of port

in England's own waters ...

Wilson continued:

Many public ships, it is true, had been built before the Armada came, and fine craft they were; but they were not enough. There was no real navy in the modern sense. The fleet which chased the Spaniards up the Channel was a volunteer fleet. Merchants had learned to defend their own cargoes.

They built fighting craft of their own to keep their coasts and harbors free of pirates, and to carry their goods over sea. They sought their fortunes as they pleased abroad, the crown annoying them with no inquiry to embarrass their search for Spanish treasure ships, or their trade in pirated linens and silks. It was this self–helping race of Englishmen ...

Wilson added:

Devonshire had the great harbor ... where a whole race of venturesome and hardy fishermen were nurtured. All the great sea names of the Elizabethan age belong to it. Drake, Hawkins, Raleigh, and the Gilberts were all Devonshire men; and it was from Plymouth that the fleet went out which beat the great Armada on its way to shipwreck in the north.

With Spain's Armada destroyed, England and Holland were now established as major European powers. Spain's monopoly of the seas, held since the time of Columbus, was ended.

Soon England, Holland, Sweden, and France rushed to stake their claims in the New World and found colonies in America. Adam Smith wrote in *The Wealth of Nations*, 1776:

The Spaniards, by virtue of the first discovery, claimed all America as their own, and ... such was ... the terror of their name, that the greater part of the other nations of Europe were afraid to establish themselves in any other part of that great continent ...

But ... the defeat ... of their Invincible Armada ... put it out of their power to obstruct any longer the settlements of the other European nations. In the course of the 17th century ... English, French, Dutch, Danes, and Swedes ... attempted to make some settlements in the new world.

In 1595, Sir Walter Raleigh set out in search of El Dorado–the City of Gold. Instead he found Pitch Lake on the Island of Trinidad–the world's largest natural asphalt lake.

Caulking the hulls of their vessels with this pitch enabled British ships to sail faster. This, together with tall pines of Maine used for masts, were critical factors aiding the British navy in becoming the most powerful navy in the world.

In 1601, King Philip III sent Spain's navy to the southern shores of Ireland and landed thousands of Spanish troops with the intention of staging an invasion of England. The Spanish were repulsed at the Siege of Kinsale, and thousands of Irish were sold into slavery and sent to the Caribbean.

After a century of Spanish explorations, early North American settlements by other countries included:

- •1607–New English Colony, with capital of Jamestown (Virginia);
- •1608–New France Colony, with capital of Quebec (Canada);
- •1624–New Dutch Colony, with capital of New Amsterdam (New York); and
- •1638–New Sweden Colony, with capital of Christina (Delaware & New Jersey).

◈

52. LIST OF EARLY 17TH CENTURY POPES

To see events of Europe in context, it is helpful to know the backdrop of the Popes during this era:

- Clement VIII, 1592–1605, organized an alliance of European Christian powers to fight The Long Turkish War (1593-1606), against the Ottoman Empire – a war in which the young English Captain John Smith fought. Clement VIII convened the Congregatio de Auxiliis addressing doctrinal disputes between Dominicans and Jesuits regarding free will and divine grace.

An account from around 1600, was that as Turks conquered west, Europeans were exposed to the Muslim drink "kahve," or "coffee," the word being derived from the Arabic word "kafir," meaning "infidel," as beans came from the Christian country of Ethiopia in Africa. Pope Clement VIII's advisers wanted him to denounce it as "the devil's drink," but upon tasting it, he supposedly declared, "This devil's drink is so good, we should cheat the devil by baptizing it." Coffee's popularity spread across Europe.

- Leo XI, April 1–27, 1605, was the nephew of Leo X, being called "Papa Lampo" (Lightning Pope) for his brief pontificate.

- Paul V, 1605–1621, was known for his building projects, including the facade of St Peter's Basilica. He established the Bank of the Holy Spirit in 1605, and restored the Aqua Traiana.

- Gregory XV, 1621–1623, established the Congregation for the Propagation of the Faith in 1622, and issued the bull Aeterni Patris in 1621 which imposed conclaves to be by secret ballot. In 1623, he issued Omnipotentis Dei against magicians and witches.

- Urban VIII, 1623–1644, held trial against Galileo Galilei. He was the last pope to enlarge papal territories by force of arms. In 1624, he issued a papal bull making the use of tobacco in holy places punishable by excommunication.

༺

53. KING JAMES I

When Elizabeth died March 24, 1603, the son of Mary–Queen of Scots, King James VI of Scotland, was officially crowned King James I of England, Ireland, Wales and Scotland.

Earlier, in 1589, James, at 23-years-old, had an arranged to marry the 14-year-old Anne of Denmark. When her ship was lost in a storm and forced to the coast of Norway, James set sail with 300 men to rescue her.

They were formally married in Oslo, Norway in 1590. On their way back to Scotland, they stopped in Copenhagen where they met the famous astronomer Tycho Brahe.

Though tutored by Scottish Presbyterians, James I rejected Presbyterian concepts of limited-government and wholeheartedly embraced "the divine right of kings," declaring:

> Kings are ... God's lieutenants upon earth ...
> sit upon God's throne ... The king is overlord
> of the whole land ... master over every person ...
> having power over the life & death of every one.

༺

54. RICHARD HAKLUYT

Richard Hakluyt (1553-1616) was chaplain to the 1st Earl of Salisbury, Robert Cecil, who was Secretary of State to Elizabeth I and James I.

Hakluyt encouraged colonizing America by writing *Divers Voyages Touching the Discoverie of America* (1582) and *The Principal Navigations, Voiages, Traffiques & Discoueries of the English Nation* (1589–1600). He translated Hernando de Soto's discoveries in Florida, and published it as *Virginia*

Richly Valued, by the Description of the Maine Land of Florida, Her Next Neighbour (1609).

Hakluyt was one of the leading investors, called adventurers, of the Charter of the Virginia Company of London, serving as a director in 1589. He was the main person petitioning James I to grant a patent permitting the colonization of Virginia, This was granted in 1606 to the London Company and Plymouth Company, together referred to as the Virginia Company.

Hakluyt solicited wealthy individuals to fund the Virginia Company. He recommended Rev. Robert Hunt to be the colony's chaplain. His writings provided resource material to authors of the day, including Shakespeare. Hakluyt's persistent advocating of colonization led Scottish historian William Robertson to write: "England is more indebted to him for its American possessions than to any man of that age."

✎

55. GOSNOLD'S VIRGINIA COLONY

Bartholomew Gosnold (1571–1607) had been an English privateer, and was friends with the major proponents of a Virginia colony: Sir Walter Raleigh, Richard Hakluyt, and Robert Cecil.

Gosnold's wife Mary was the granddaughter of Sir Andrew Judd, the Lord Mayor of London. His family was friends with Sir Francis Bacon.

Many English investors were interested only in colonizing parts of Ireland, but others sought to colonize the New World.

Monarchs did not finance colonizing enterprises, but, in exchanged for a percentage of the return, granted monopoly privileges to individuals or corporations who undertook the risks. Colonizers approached wealthy individuals to raise venture capital. One investor in the Virginia Company was the Earl of Southampton, who also helped finance Shakespeare.

It was difficult to get investors as Sir Walter Raleigh lost a fortune on his failed Roanoke Colony. It was a decade before another venture was attempted. Though Raleigh still technically held the patent from Queen Elizabeth for colonizing, he had not brought in any money, so Gosnold was allowed to try.

Gosnold led the first expedition to the Massachusetts area in 1602, having heard about the abundance of fish which could be sold in English markets. He arrived at Cape Elizabeth, present-day Maine, in May of 1602. He sailed south to Provincetown, where he gave Cape Cod its name. Gosnold named the island of Martha's Vineyard after his infant daughter that died.

He established a small post on the secluded Cuttyhunk Island, Massachusetts, but settlers abandoned it before winter, fearing the scarcity of supplies. There is still a monument to Bartholomew Gosnold on shore of Cuttyhunk. Gosnold returned to England.

Gosnold wanted to try one more time. He and other organizers reputedly conceived the idea for what became the successful Virginia Company Colony around the fireplace of his home, called Otley Hall, which still stands in the rolling countryside of Suffolk, and is considered one England's top 20 historic houses.

Gosnold approached the King for exclusive permission, and in 1606, King James granted him the Virginia Company Charter:

> Greatly commending ... their desires for the Furtherance of so noble a Work, which may, by the Providence of Almighty God, hereafter tend to the Glory of His Divine Majesty, in propagating of Christian Religion to such People, as yet live in Darkness and miserable Ignorance of the true Knowledge and Worship of God.

Gosnold recruited notable individuals, including Captain John Smith, renown for fighting in the Long Turkish War. Setting sail in late 1606, Gosnold was captain of one of the three ships, the *Godspeed;* Christopher Newport was captain of the *Susan Constant*; and John Ratcliffe was captain of the *Discovery*.

After a five month journey, which included a stop in Puerto Rico, they entered Chesapeake Bay and made landfall on April 26, 1607 at Cape Henry, named for Prince Henry of Wales.

Upon disembarking, the settlers' first act was to erect a Christian cross. Their chaplain, Rev. Robert Hunt, offered prayer, as portrayed in the CBN film *First Landing the Movie* (2007 Award of Excellence Winner, Michael Little, executive producer).

Sailing up the James River, named after King James, on May 13, 1607, they established Jamestown—the first permanent English settlement in the New World.

Bartholomew Gosnold helped design Jamestown, but died after only four months, on August 22, 1607, being buried outside the fort. Gosnold's brother accompanied them on the voyage, but he drowned in a storm, trying to cross Boston Harbor to Hog Island (present-day Spinnaker Island.)

John Smith described the early Jamestown settlement in *Advertisements for Unexperienced Planters*, published in London, 1631:

> When I first went to Virginia, I well remember, we did hang an awning (which is an old sail) to three or four trees to shadow us from the sun, our walls were rails of wood, our seats unhewn trees, till we cut planks, our Pulpit a bar of wood nailed to two neighboring trees, in foul weather we shifted into an old rotten tent, for we had few better ... this was our Church, till we built a homely thing like a barn ...

We had daily Common Prayer morning and evening, every day two Sermons, and every three months the holy Communion, till our Minister (Robert Hunt) died, but our Prayers daily, with an Homily on Sundays.

Settlers wrote of Rev. Robert Hunt:

1607. To the glory of God and in memory of the Reverend Robert Hunt, Presbyter, appointed by the Church of England. Minister of the Colony which established the English Church and English Civilization at Jamestown ...

His people, members of the Colony, left this testimony concerning him. Rev. Robert Hunt was an honest, religious and courageous Divine.

He preferred the Service of God in so good a voyage to every thought of ease at home.

Settlers continued their tribute of Rev. Robert Hunt:

He endured every privation, yet none ever heard him repine. During his life our factions were ofte healed, and our greatest extremities so comforted that they seemed easy in comparison with what we endured after his memorable death.

We all received from him the Holy Communion together, as a pledge of reconciliation, for we all loved him for his exceeding goodness. He planted the first Protestant Church in America and laid down his life in the foundation of America.

In the next three years, Jamestown settlers experienced malaria from mosquito filled swamps, exposure, and Indian attacks. They suffered a "starving time" during the winter of 1609–1610, where, at the beginning of winter there were 500 inhabitants, by spring, there were only 60.

In 1610, the remaining settlers decided to abandon

Jamestown, but just as they were leaving, Thomas West, 3rd Baron Delaware, arrived with supplies, June 10, 1610. He had a commission to serve as the colony's governor, and prevented settlers from giving up.

In 1613, Virginia governor, Sir Samuel Argall, raided and destroyed the French Jesuit colony of Saint–Sauveur on Mount Desert Island (now in Maine). He burned the buildings on Sainte–Croix (now in Maine) and the possession of the Port Royal (now in Nova Scotia). Argall also kidnapped Pocahontas.

᥁

56. CAPTAIN JOHN SMITH

Most Americans are aware of Captain John Smith's role in the founding of Jamestown, but he had an eventful career prior, as recorded in *The True Travels, Adventures and Observations of Captain John Smith in Europe, Asia, Africa and America*, (1630).

Six years before sailing to America, Smith joined Austrian forces and fought in The Long Turkish War (1593-1606) against the Ottomans invading Hungary.

Mehmed III (1566–1603) became Ottoman Sultan in 1595. He had his 16 brothers strangled to death to eliminate rivalry to his throne. Bertrand Russell, who received the Nobel Prize for Literature, stated in his Nobel Lecture, 1950:

> Over and over again in Mohammedan history, dynasties have come to grief because the sons of a sultan by different mothers could not agree, and in the resulting civil war universal ruin resulted.

Sultan Mehmed III raised an army of 60,000 and in 1596 conquered the Hungarian city of Erlau. He defeated the Austrian Habsburg and Transylvanian forces at the Battle of Mezõkeresztes.

The Complete Works of Captain John Smith,

1580–1631 (edited by Philip L. Barbour, Institute of Early American History & Culture, UNC Press, 1986) reported that at age 21, John Smith joined the ranks of Austrian Hapsburg Earl of Meldritch, assigned to the General of Artillery, Baron Kisell.

Charles Dudley Warner, of *Harper's Magazine,* wrote in *Captain John Smith* (1881, chap. 2–3), of Smith marching with Germans, Austrians, French, and Hungarians to repel Turks who had captured Budapest and invaded Lower Hungary, Wallachia, Moldovia, Romania and Transylvania near the Black Sea.

In 1600–1601, during the campaign of Romanian Prince Michael the Brave, Smith introduced ingenious battle tactics. Duromg the Turkish siege of a garrison at Oberlymback, he devised a method of signaling messages with torches, and using gunpowder to create diversions. The resulting victory earned him the rank of captain with a command of 250 horsemen.

At the siege of Alba Regalis, Smith assisted Duc de Mercoeur by devising makeshift bombs of earthen pots filled with gunpowder, musket shot and covered with pitch, and catapulted them into the city, leading to an evacuation.

The city of Regall fell, located in a pass between Hungary and Transylvania, "the Turks having ornamented the walls with Christian heads when they captured the fortress." Smith led an effort to regain the city, fighting under General Moyses, who served the Prince of Transylvania, Sigismund Bathory.

During a lull in the fighting, the bashaw (officer) of the Turks put out a challenge. In a "David and Goliath" style contest, the 23–year–old John Smith was chosen to fight. He defeated the bashaw, cutting off his head.

To avenge the bashaw's death, another Muslim challenged Smith, and he also lost his head. This happened a third time, resulting in Smith being awarded a "coat-of-arms" by Prince Sigismund Bathory, depicting three severed turbaned heads.

General Moyses, with Captain John Smith, recaptured Regall, then Veratis, Solmos and Kapronka.

Smith then served in the regiment of Earl Meldritch, fighting in 1602 for Radu Serban, to defend Wallachia against invading Turks. In the battle, the Earl of Meldritch was killed, along with 30,000 soldiers. John Smith was wounded and left for dead:

> Smith among the slaughtered dead bodies, and many a gasping soul with toils and wounds lay groaning among the rest, till being found by the pillagers he was able to live, and perceiving by his armor and habit, his ransom might be better than his death, they led him prisoner with many others.

Smith was taken to Axopolis and sold with other prisoners at the slave market to Bashaw Bogall, "so chained by the necks in gangs of twenty they marched to Constantinople." The Bashaw Bogall's mistress had pity on Smith and sent him to her brother, Tymor Bashaw. Unfortunately, the brother "diverted all this to the worst cruelty," stripped Smith naked, shaved him bald, riveted an iron ring around his neck, clothed him in goat skins, and, as slave of slaves, gave him only goat entrails to eat.

Following a beating received while thrashing in a field, Smith seized the opportunity to kill his master and hide his body in the straw. He put on his master's clothes, took a bag of grain, and rode off toward Russia.

After 16 days he reached a Muscovite garrison on the River Don, where the iron ring was removed from his neck. With their help, he found his way through Poland back to his troops in Transylvania.

After being released from service with a large reward, Smith traveled through Europe to Morocco in Northern Africa to fight Muslim Barbary pirates in the Mediterranean Sea. In 1605, at the age of 26, he returned to England.

In 1606, Captain John Smith set sail to help found Jamestown, Virginia, the first permanent English colony in North America. In 1607, Chief Powhatan was about to kill Smith, but he was saved through the pleadings of his 11–year–old daughter Pocahontas. Smith wrote in *New England's Trials* (1622):

> God made Pocahontas, the King's daughter
> the means to deliver me.

In 1614, six years before the Pilgrims arrived, Smith explored Maine and Massachusetts Bay.

∽

57. POCAHONTAS

Pocahontas (c.1595-March 1617) was daughter of Chief Powhatan. In 1607, she befriended the English settlers of the Jamestown Colony. In March of 1613, she was kidnapped by Captain Samuel Argall.

After being instructed in the Christian faith, Pocahontas was baptized, taking the name Rebekah. The painting of this, by John Gadsby Chapman, 1839, is in the National Portrait Gallery of the Smithsonian Institution, and a copy hangs in the U.S. Capitol Rotunda. The inscription painted on the portrait reads:

> Matoaks ats Rebecka, daughter to the mighty Prince Powhatan Emperour of Attanoughkonmouck ats Virginia converted and baptized in the Christian faith, and wife to the wor. Mr. Tho:Rolff.

Reverend Richard Bucke, second chaplain to the Virginia Colony, presided over her marriage in 1614, to John Rolfe, the council member of the Jamestown settlement noted for having introduced tobacco cultivation. Rolfe, a widower ten years her senior, asked Jamestown officials for permission to marry her:

> Pokanhuntas to whom my hartie and best thoughts are, and have for along time been so intangled, and inthralled in so intricate a laborinth.

John and Pocahontas moved to England, where she was received as royalty. They had a son, Thomas, whose descendants include statesmen, educators and ministers, the most notable being John Randolph of Roanoke and Edith Bolling Galt, who married President Woodrow Wilson in 1915.

In 1617, Pocahontas contracted smallpox in England and died. Her last words were: "Tis enough that the child liveth."

❧

58. CHURCH OF ENGLAND

The Church of England was established as the official denomination in Virginia from 1606 till 1786.

Webster's 1828 Dictionary defined "establishment" of religion as:

> The episcopal form of religion, so called in England.

Thomas Jefferson wrote in his *Autobiography*, 1821:

> The first settlers of Virginia were Englishmen, loyal subjects to their King and Church, and the grant to Sir Walter Raleigh contained an express proviso that their laws "should not be against the true Christian faith, now professed in the Church of England."

The Second Charter of Virginia, May 23, 1609, stated:

> The principal Effect which we can expect or desire of this Action is the Conversion and reduction of the people in those parts unto the true worship of God and the Christian Religion ...

It shall be necessary for all such our loving Subjects ... to live together, in the Fear and true Worship of Almighty God, Christian Peace, and civil Quietness, with each other.

The Third Charter of Virginia, March 12, 1611, stated:

Our loving Subjects ... for the Propagation of Christian Religion, and Reclaiming of People barbarous, to Civility and Humanity, We have ... granted unto them ... the first Colony in Virginia.

Virginia House of Burgesses, July 30, 1619, narrative of Speaker of the House, John Pory:

But, forasmuch as men's affairs do little prosper when God's service is neglected, all the Burgesses took their places in the quire (choir) till prayer was said by Mr. Bucke, the Minister, that it would please God to guide and sanctify all our proceedings to His own glory, and the good of this plantation.

Prayer being ended, to the intent that as we had begun at God Almighty so we might proceed awful and due respect toward his lieutenant ... for laying a surer foundation for the conversion of the Indians to Christian religion ...

All ministers shall duly read Divine service and exercise their ministerial function according to the ecclesiastical laws and orders of the Church of England.

Virginia House of Burgesses, August 4, 1619, narrative of Jamestown:

All ministers shall duly read Divine service, and exercise their ministerial function according to the Ecclesiastical laws and orders of the Church of England, and every Sunday in the afternoon shall Catechize such as are not yet ripe to come to the Communion.

And whosoever of them shall be found negligent or faulty in this kind shall be subject to the censure of the Governor and Council of Estate.

The Ministers and Churchwardens shall seek to present all ungodly disorders, the committers whereof if, upon good admonitions and mild reproof, they will not forebear the said scandalous offenses, as suspicions of whoredoms, dishonest company keeping with women and such like, they are to be presented and punished accordingly.

If any person after two warnings, do not amend his or her life in point of evident suspicion of incontinency or of the commission of any other enormous sins, that then he or she be presented by the Churchwardens and suspended for a time from the Church by the minister.

In which Interim if the same person do not amend and humbly submit him or herself to the Church, he is then fully to be excommunicate and soon after a writ or warrant to be sent from the Governor for the apprehending of his person and seizing on all his goods ...

All persons whatsoever upon the Sabbath day shall frequent Divine service and sermons both forenoon and afternoon, and all such as bear arms shall bring their pieces, swords, powder and shot.

And everyone that shall transgress this law shall forfeit three shillings a time to the use of the Church, all lawful and necessary impediments excepted. But if a servant in this case shall willfully neglect his Master's command he shall suffer bodily punishment.

On December 4, 1619, 38 colonists who landed in Virginia at a place called Berkeley Hundred, writing:

We ordain that the day of our ship's arrival ... in the land of Virginia shall be yearly and perpetually kept Holy as a day of Thanksgiving to Almighty God.

Virginia House of Burgesses, August 3, 1621, ordinances of Jamestown:

> We ... charge ... they ... assist .... in the service of God, and the enlargement of his Kingdom amongst the heathen people; and next, in erecting of the said Colony ... in maintaining the said people in justice and Christian conversation amongst themselves.

Virginia Colony, March 22, 1622, was able to avert a threatened Indian attack due to the warning of a young Indian named "Chanco," as memorialized on a marker:

> In memory of Chanco, an Indian youth converted to Christianity, who resided in the household of Richard Pace across the river from Jamestown and who, on the eve of the Indian massacre of March 22, 1622, warned Pace of the murderous plot thus enabling Pace to cross the river in a canoe to alert and save the Jamestown settlement from impending disaster.

Virginia House of Burgesses, 1623, ordinance of Jamestown, required civil magistrates:

> To see that the Sabbath was not profaned by working or any employments, or journeying from place to place.

Virginia House of Burgesses, March 5, 1624, ordinances of Jamestown:

> 1. That there shall be in every plantation, where the people use to meet for the worship of God, a house or room sequestered for that purpose ...

> 2. That whosoever shall absent himself from Divine service any Sunday without an allowable excuse shall forfeit a pound of tobacco ...

> 3. That there be an uniformity in our Church

as near as may be to the Canons in England ...
and that all persons yield ready obedience unto
them under pain of censure.

In 1668, the Virginia House of Burgesses in
Jamestown passed an ordinance stating:

> The 27th of August appointed for a Day of
> Humiliation, Fasting and Prayer, to implore
> God's mercy: if any person be found upon
> that day gaming, drinking, or working (works
> of necessity excepted), upon presentment by
> church–wardens and proof, he shall be fined
> one hundred pounds of tobacco.

In 1699, the Virginia Assembly adopted the
statutes of Monarchs William and Mary allowing for
the toleration of some Protestant dissenters. James
Madison wrote to Robert Walsh, March 2, 1819:

> The English Church was originally the established
> religion ... Of other sects there were but few adherents,
> except the Presbyterians who predominated on the
> west side of the Blue Mountains.

Colonial Virginia had an "establishment" of the
Anglican or Church of England, from 1606 to 1786.

Establishment meant:

- •mandatory membership;
- •mandatory taxes to support it; and
- •no one could hold public office unless they
  were a member.

Over time, lax enforcement allowed "dissenting"
religious groups to enter Virginia, the first being
Presbyterians and Quakers, followed by German
Lutherans, Mennonites, Moravian Brethren, and Baptists.

❧

59. THE IMPORTANCE OF COMPANIES

Virginia was originally a "company" colony. The
history of the development of "companies" is significant.

When Muslim Turks conquered the land trade routes from Europe to Asia, Europeans attempted to find sea routes, financed either by kings or wealthy private individuals, as there were no "companies."

There were merchant guilds, craft guilds, and religious guilds, but they did not have large amounts of capital. The reason there were not companies in the Middle Ages was because the paying and receiving of interest was considered "the sin of usury."

After the Reformation, Protestant countries formed the first "joint–stock" companies. A "joint–stock" company was much like modern-day crowd–sourcing or crowd–funding, such as Kickstarter or GoFundMe, where an individual, such as carpenters, blacksmiths, bakers, masons, etc., could invest in a ship sailing to the Far East, and when it returned full of valuable spices, they would receive a profit.

The investor only risked what the amount invested. There was no additional liability for any losses associated with the company. Kings would grant royal charter monopoly rights to limited–liability joint stock companies in exchange for a portion of the return.

After the Reformation, what is considered the first modern joint–stock company was England's Company of Merchant Adventurers to New Lands, given a charter from King Edward VI in 1553. It attempted to find a northeast sea route from England over the top of Russia to reach China, India and Indonesia's Spice Islands.

The 240 shareholders invested enough money to outfit three ships, but sailing north of Russia, two ships became trapped in ice and the crews froze to death.

The company transitioned into the Muscovy Company, being granted a charter by Mary I in 1555, with the purpose of opening up trade with Moscow and Russia's Czar Ivan the Terrible.

In 1581, England started the Levant Company for the purpose of trading with Turkey's Ottoman Muslims. The British East India Company was charted by Queen Elizabeth I on December 31, 1600.

Virginia's Roanoke Colony was personally financed by Sir Walter Raleigh and his half-brother, Sir Humphrey Gilbert, who drowned in 1583 trying to colonize St. John's, Newfoundland. The Roanoke Colony failed, being called "The Lost Colony."

In 1606, King James I granted a new charter to the Virginia Company of London, but it suffered such tremendous financial losses due to diseases, famine and Indian massacres, that the colony was surrendered to the King, who made it a Royal Crown Colony in 1624.

European companies traded with outposts in Africa, the Mediterranean and America. Merchants, sailors, and colonizers struggled to balance two competing motivations, namely, gold versus the gospel.

≈

60. DUTCH EAST INDIA COMPANY

In 1595, Dutch merchant–explorer Jan Huyghen van Linschoten published *Travel Accounts of Portuguese Navigation in the Orient*, which included highly guarded secret nautical maps. The circulation of this book ended Portugal's monopoly on Asian sea trade.

The Dutch East India Company (Verenigde Oost–Indische Compagnie) was founded in 1602, being the first intercontinental trade corporation with limited liability. Bakers, blacksmiths, cooks, farmers, etc., could invest in a ship going to the Far East and when it came back filled with spices, porcelain china, or other valuable goods, the investors would be paid a profit, interest, or "dividends."

Individuals could trade their shares of stock at what became the Amsterdam Stock Exchange–the first of its kind in the world. In case ships sank or were captured, such as by Muslim Barbary pirates, the Dutch invented the first modern insurance companies to cover losses.

By 1612, the Dutch East India Company had become the most profitable company, eclipsing in profits all the companies of other nations combined for nearly two centuries.

The Dutch experienced the first stock market crash with the Tulip Mania of 1636–1637. Tulips were imported from Turkey and became so popular that a single tulip bulb was worth more than an average person's yearly salary. Suddenly, when they began to bloom, tulips bulbs dropped in one day to one-hundredth of their previous value, plunging the country into an economic depression.

The Dutch captured Goa, India, from the Portuguese and opened trade with Jakarta, Mauritius and the Indonesian Spice Island of Maluku. They had a monopoly on trade with Japan for centuries.

They sighted Fiji and Australia, and established colonies around the world, from Africa to Asia, including Tasmania, New Zealand, Jakarta, and Java.

The Dutch and the English fought many battles over control of Far East territories whose profitable exports included: coffee, sugar, indigo (blue dye) and opium. As the British gained control of India, the Dutch gained control over Indonesia.

Trade was interrupted when the volcano Tambora erupted on Sumbawa in 1815, and again in 1883, when the volcano Krakatoa erupted on Java – the blast from which was heard 3,000 miles away, being considered the world's loudest sound. Tsunami waves were over 150 feet high and ash devastated the global climate for over a year.

Another threat to Dutch trade was Wahhabi Islam.

As early as 1804, there were reports of Muslim pilgrims returning from Mecca to the Far East infected with militant Wahhabi teaching. Called "Padri," their prominent leader, Tuanu Imam Bonjol, advocated sharia law and violently overthrowing governments. Many natives fled to the Dutch for protection during the Padri War of 1821–1838. Order was restored when the Dutch arrested the imams who were inciting violence.

Eventually, Dutch leaders took an ethical position regarding the welfare of the native inhabitants of their colonies. One such leader was Abraham Kuyper, who founded the Reformed Churches of the Netherlands in 1892, and was elected Prime Minister of the Netherlands in 1901. Kuyper wrote pamphlets promoting the moral responsibility of the Dutch to care for the people of Java, which was experiencing a famine.

᪥

61. THE ENGLISH BIBLE

As mentioned earlier, in England, John Wycliffe translated the earliest version of the English Bible in 1380. His teachings inspired other early reformers, such John Hus in Prague. This was over seventy years before Gutenberg's invention of the printing press in 1454.

In 1525, William Tyndale began printing an English translation of the New Testament. Henry VIII ordered him hunted down and arrested. Tyndale was strangled and burnt at the stake on October 6, 1536. His last words were, "Lord, open the King of England's eyes."

In 1535, Myles Coverdale, relying heavily on William Tyndale's translation, printed the first complete English Bible.

Franklin Roosevelt stated on the 400th Anniversary of the Printing of the English Bible, October 6, 1935:

> The four hundredth anniversary of the printing of the first English Bible is an event

of great significance ... The ... influence of this greatest of books ... so greatly affected the progress of Christian civilization ...

This Book continues to hold its unchallenged place as the most loved, the most quoted and the most universally read and pondered of all the volumes ... It continues to hold its supreme place as the Book of books ...

We cannot read the history of our rise and development as a Nation, without reckoning with the place the Bible has occupied in shaping the advances of the Republic ... Its teaching ... is ploughed into the very heart of the race.

Where we have been truest and most consistent in obeying its precepts we have attained the greatest measure of contentment and prosperity."

After Henry VIII broke from Rome in 1534, his advisers suggested that to finalize this break, England should stop using Rome's Latin Bible, and instead use an English Bible, similar to German Protestant countries which used Martin Luther's German translation.

Henry liked the idea, and in 1537, he permitted John Rogers to print the Matthew–Tyndale Bible, but it was not disseminated to the population at large.

In 1539, Anglican Archbishop of Canterbury Thomas Crammer hired Myles Coverdale to publish the "Great Bible." Being authorized by Henry VIII, it was the first English Bible officially approved for public use.

Convinced it would solidify his break with Rome, Henry had the Great Bible distributed to every church in England. Being extremely valuable, it was chained to pulpits, yet available for people to read. This occurred three years after William Tyndale's prayer before being martyred, "Lord, open the King of England's eyes."

As the Great Bible spread around England, it produced an unanticipated result – people began to read it. As they did, they began to compared what was in it to the personal and political behavior of Henry VIII. This birthed a movement to "purify" the Church of England. Those in the movement were called "Puritans." The King did not think he needed "purifying," so he persecuted them.

When Henry VIII's daughter "Bloody Mary" persecuted Puritans, many fled to Geneva, Switzerland, where they printed the Geneva Bible in 1560. This was the first Bible with numbered verses.

For nearly a century, the Geneva Bible was the most popular English Bible, being quoted by William Shakespeare in plays, and by John Bunyan in *Pilgrims Progress*. Being the favorite of the Puritans, it was the first Bible brought to America by the Pilgrims.

The Geneva Bible was only reluctantly tolerated by Elizabeth I, as its many Calvinist marginal notes were critical of monarchy.

After the Counter-Reformation began, the Roman Catholic Church published the Douay–Rheims English Version, based on the Latin Vulgate, in 1589.

With so many different translations, King James decided to publish a translation to end all translations, and which would be void of controversial marginal notes.

Beginning in 1604, a team of 47 scholars worked for seven years to produce the King James Bible of 1611. Selling billions of copies, it has since become the most best-selling book of all time.

Woodrow Wilson stated in Denver, Colorado, at the Tercentenary Celebration of the King James Translation of the Bible, May 7, 1911:

> I wonder how many persons in this great audience realize the significance for English–

speaking peoples of the translation of the Bible into the English tongue.

Up to the time of the translation of the Bible into English, it was a book for long ages withheld from the perusal of the peoples of other languages ... and not a little of the history of liberty lies in the circumstance that the moving sentences of this book were made familiar to the ears and the understanding of those peoples who have led mankind in exhibiting the forms of government and the impulses of reform which have made for freedom and for self-government among mankind ...

Wilson added:

For this is a book which reveals men unto themselves, not as creatures in bondage, not as men under human authority, not as those bidden to take counsel and command of any human source.

It reveals every man to himself as a distinct moral agent, responsible not to men, not even to those men whom he has put over him in authority, but responsible through his own conscience to his Lord and Maker.

Whenever a man sees this vision he stands up a free man, whatever may be the government under which he lives, if he sees beyond the circumstances of his own life ...

Wilson continued:

We must look upon the Bible as the great charter of the human soul – as the "Magna Charta" of the human soul.

You know the interesting circumstances which gave rise to the Magna Charta ... at Runnymede ... how the barons of England, representing the people of England ... met upon that historic spot and parleyed with John, the King. They said …

"There are certain inalienable rights of English–speaking men which you must observe. They are not given by you, they can not be taken away by you. Sign your name here to this parchment upon which these rights are written and we are your subjects. Refuse to put your name to this document and we are your sworn enemies. Here are our swords to prove it" …

This is the meaning of this charter of the human soul …

That is the reason that the Bible has stood at the back of progress. That is the reason that reform has come not from the top but from the bottom. If you are ever tempted to let a government reform itself, I ask you to look back in the pages of history and find me a government that reformed itself …

Wilson concluded:

America was born a Christian nation. America was born to exemplify that devotion to the elements of righteousness which are derived from the revelations of Holy Scripture ...

The destiny of America lies in their daily perusal of this great book of revelations – that if they would see America free and pure they will make their own spirits free and pure by this baptism of the Holy Scripture.

❧

62. RELIGIOUS UNIFORMITY

In England–YES, people could read the Bible in their own language,–but NO, people could not believe whatever they wanted. Parliament passed the Act of Uniformity of 1558, requiring all persons to attend the Anglican Church once a week or be fined 12 pence, a considerable sum for the poor.

The Act required use of the English Book of Common Prayer and set the order of prayer. It was a crime punishable by fines and imprisonment to conduct unofficial services.

In 1593, Puritan separatists Henry Barrowe and John Greenwood were found guilty of violating the Act of Uniformity and were executed. Catholics, called "Papists," were also found guilty of violating the Act.

King James I demanded religious uniformity or he would "harry them out of the land."

During the reign of King Charles I, Anglican Archbishop William Laud was obsessed with uniformity. In office 1633–1640, he published a new *Book of Common Prayer* to standardize worship, derogatorily called "Laud's liturgy." He sent spies, like IRS agents, into churches to enforce observance.

Laud purged academia of all Puritans and in 1625 compiled a list of churchmen, placing an "O" for Orthodox beside the names of those to be promoted, and a "P" for Puritan of those not to be.

The Test Act of 1673 barred non-Anglicans from office by requiring public officials to receive the sacraments in the Church of England. Voltaire wrote in *Letters Concerning the English Nation* (1733):

> No one can hold office in England or in Ireland unless he is a faithful Anglican.

Another group gave up hope of trying to "purify" the Church of England. They were called "separatists" because they met in secret, at night, by candlelight, in barns and basements, similar to illegal house churches in China, North Korea, or Saudi Arabia.

These separatists were punished by being put in stocks, whipped, imprisoned or even branded as heretics. Though not as severe as Islamic sharia law, it is difficult for modern society to imagine the abuse of power which occurs when religious leaders are under the control of a government which demands uniformity.

᪥

63. PILGRIMS' TRIALS & PERSECUTIONS

One of the separatist leaders in England was William Brewster, who, beginning in 1606, arranged for the small Pilgrim congregation to meet privately, in secret, at the Scrooby manor house. Richard Clifton was their pastor, John Robinson was a teacher, and William Brewster was the presiding elder.

Brewster was fined the equivalent of thousands of dollars for non-compliance with the church. He was pressured to resign from his prestigious postmaster position and the group considered fleeing to Amsterdam. Pilgrim Governor William Bradford wrote of this in *Of Plymouth Plantation*:

> Mr. Brewster went and lived in the country ... till the Lord revealed Himself further to him.
>
> In the end, the tyranny of the bishops against godly preachers and people, in silencing the former and persecuting the latter, caused him and many more to look further into things, and to realize the unlawfulness of their episcopal callings, and to feel the burden of their many anti-christian corruptions, which both he and they endeavored to throw off ...
>
> After they had joined themselves together in communion, as was mentioned earlier, he was a special help and support to them.
>
> On the Lord's day they generally met at his house, which was a manor of the bishop's, and he entertained them with great kindness when they came, providing for them at heavy expense to himself.
>
> He was the leader of those who were

captured at Boston in Lincolnshire, suffering the greatest loss, and was one of the seven who were kept longest in prison and afterwards bound over to the assizes.

It was illegal to leave England without permission. On their first attempt in 1607, they were arrested at Scotia Creek. On their second attempt, in 1608, they successfully left from the Humber and arrived in Holland. William Bradford recounted:

> But after these things they could not long continue in any peaceable condition, but were hunted and persecuted on every side, so as their former afflictions were but as flea–bitings in comparison of these which now came upon them.

> For some were taken and clapped up in prison, others had their houses beset and watched night and day, and hardly escaped their hands; and ye most were fain to fly and leave their houses and habitations, and the means of their livelihood.

Bradford explained how some Pilgrims bought passage on a ship to sail to Holland, but right before it departed, the ship master robbed and arrested them:

> There was a large company of them purposed to get passage at Boston in Lincolnshire, and for that end had hired a ship wholly to themselves, and made agreement with the master to be ready at a certain day, and take them and their goods in, at a convenient place, where they accordingly would all attend in readiness.

> So after long waiting, and large expenses, though he kept not day with them, yet he came at length and took them in, in the night.

> But when he had them and their goods aboard, he betrayed them, having before hand plotted with the searchers and other officers so

to do; who took them, and put them into open boats, and there rifled and ransacked them, searching them to their shirts for money, yea even the women further then became modesty;

and then carried them back into the town, and made them a spectacle and wonder to the multitude, which came flocking on all sides to behold them.

Being thus first, by the chatch-poule (tax collector) officers, rifled, and striped of their money, books, and much other goods, they were presented to the magistrates, and messengers sent to inform the lords of the Counsel of them; and so they were committed to ward.

Indeed the magistrates used them courteously, and shewed them what favor they could; but could not deliver them, till order came from the Counsel-table.

But the issue was that after a month's imprisonment, the greatest part were dismissed, and sent to the places from whence they came; but seven of the principal were still kept in prison, and bound over to the assizes (justice of the peace).

Bradford gave the account of Pilgrims who arranged for a Dutch ship to meet them at a secluded shoreline:

The next spring after, there was another attempt made by some of these and others, to get over at an other place.

And it so fell out, that they light of a Dutch-man at Hull, having a ship of his own belonging to Zealand; they made agreement with him, and acquainted him with their condition, hoping to find more faithfulness in him, then in the former of their own nation.

He bad them not fear, for he would do well enough. He was by appointment to take them in between Grimsby and Hull, where was a large (sea shore) a good way distant from any town.

Unfortunately, the Pilgrims arrived a day early. While waiting all day in a bark (boat), the women and children became sick and waited by a creek:

> Now against the prefixed time, the women and children, with the goods, were sent to the place in a small bark, which they had hired for that end; and the men were to meet them by land. But it so fell out, that they were there a day before the ship came, and the sea being rough, and the women very sick, prevailed with the seamen to put into a creek hard by, where they lay on ground at low water.

As the men were storing family belongings on board, an armed mob suddenly came over the hill. Despite their pleadings, the Dutch ship master pulled anchor and sailed away, leaving the women and children to be captured:

> The next morning the ship came ... the ship master, perceiving how the matter was, sent his boat to be getting the men aboard whom he saw ready, walking about the shore.
>
> But after the first boat full was got aboard, and she was ready to go for more, the ship master espied a great company, both horse and foot, with ... weapons; for the country was raised to take them.
>
> The Dutch-man seeing that, swore his countries oath, "sacrament," and having the wind fair, weighed his anchor, hoisted sails, and sailed away ... The poor men which were got aboard were in great distress for their wives and children, which they saw thus to be taken, and were left destitute of their help ...
>
> It drew tears from their eyes, and anything they had they would have given to have been

a shore again; but all in vain, there was no remedy, they must thus sadly part.

And afterward endured a fearful storm at sea, being 14 days or more before they arrived at their port, in 7 whereof they neither saw son, moon, nor stars, and were driven near the coast of Norway; the mariners themselves often despairing of life ... with shrieks and cries ... sinking without recovery.

But when man's hope and help wholly failed, the Lord's power and mercy appeared in their recovery; for the ship rose again, and gave the mariners courage again to manage her ... and in the end brought them to their desired Haven.

The women and children left in England were sent from one court to another for nearly two years till a judge told them to go home. When informed they had sold their homes, the judge put them on a ship and sent them to Holland to be joyously reunited with their husbands:

But to return to the others where we left ... pitiful it was to see the heavy case of these poor women in this distress; what weeping and crying ore every side, some for their husbands, that were carried away in the ship as is before related; others not knowing what should become of them, and their little ones; others again melted in tears, seeing their poor little ones hanging about them, crying for fear, and quaking with could.

Being thus apprehended, they were hurried from one place to another, and from one justice to another, till in the end they knew not what to do with them; for to imprison so many women and innocent children for no other cause ...

but that they must go with their husbands, seemed to be unreasonable ... and to send them home again was as difficult, for they alleged, as the truth was, they had no homes to go to, for they had either sold, or otherwise disposed of their houses and livings.

To be short, after they had been thus turmoiled a good while, and conveyed from one constable to another, they were glad to be rid of them in the end upon any terms; for all were wearied and tired with them.

Though in the mean time they (poor souls) endured misery enough; and thus in the end necessity forced a way for them ...

Their cause became famous, and occasioned many to look into the same; and their godly carriage and Christian behavior was such as left a deep impression in the minds of many ...

And in the end, notwithstanding all these storms of opposition, they all got over (to Holland) at length, some at one time and some at are other, and some in one place and some in are other, and met together again according to their desires, with no small rejoicing.

Governor Bradford wrote in *Of Plymouth Plantation*:

It is well known unto ye godly and judicious how since ye first breaking out of ye light of ye gospel in our Honorable Nation of England, (which was ye first of nations whom ye Lord adorned there with, after the gross darkness ... which had covered and overspread ye Christian world), what wars and oppositions ever since, Satan, hath raised, maintained, and continued against the Saints, from time to time, in one sort or other.

Some times by bloody death and cruel torments; other whiles imprisonments, banishments, and other hard usages; as being loath his kingdom should go down, and truth prevail, and ye churches of God revert to their ancient purity and recover their primitive order, liberty, and beauty.

But when he could not prevail by these means against the main truths of ye gospel, but that they began to take rooting in many places, being watered by ye blood of ye martyrs, and blessed from heaven with a gracious increase; he then began to take him to his ancient stratagem used of old against the first Christians.

That when by ye bloody and barbarous persecutions of ye heathen Emperors, he could not stop and subvert the course of ye Gospel, but that it speedily overspread with a wonderful celerity (speed) the then best known parts ...ye professors themselves, (working upon their pride and ambition, with other corrupt passions incident to all mortal men, yea to ye saints themselves in some measure), by which woeful effects followed; as not only bitter contentions, and heart-burnings, schisms, with other horrible confusions, but Satan took occasion and advantage thereby to foist in a number of vile ... cannons and decrees, which have since been as snares to many poor and peaceable souls even to this day. So as in ye ancient times, the persecutions by ye heathen and their Emperors, was not greater than of the Christians one against another.

⤜⤙

64. PILGRIMS IN LEIDEN

Bradford wrote of the Pilgrims departure to Holland:

Being thus constrained to leave their native soil and country, their lands and livings, and all their friends and familiar acquaintance ... to go into a country they knew not (but by hearsay) where they must learn a new language, and get their livings they knew not how, it being a dear place, and subject to the miseries of war, it was by many thought an adventure almost desperate, a case intolerable, and a misery worse than death ...

But these things did not dismay them (though they did sometimes trouble them) for their desires were sett on ye ways of God and to enjoy His ordinances; but they rested in His providence, and knew whom they had believed.

Once in Holland, the Pilgrims settled in the city of Leiden, where elder William Brewster taught English at Leiden University. Bradford wrote of Brewster:

After he came to Holland he suffered much hardship, having spent most of his means ... Towards the latter part of those twelve years spent in Holland, his circumstances improved ... for through his knowledge of Latin he was able to teach many foreign students English.

By his method they acquired it quickly and with great fluency, for he drew up rules to learn it by, after the manner of teaching Latin; and many gentlemen, both Danes and Germans, came to him, some of them being sons of distinguished men.

After several years, Pastor John Robinson and William Brewster made request to settle in Virginia by sending Articles to the Counsel of England in 1618:

Article III. The King's Majesty we acknowledge for Supreme Governor in his Dominion ... but in all things obedience is due unto him if the thing commanded be not against God's Word ...

Article VII. And lastly, we desire to give unto all Superiors due honor to preserve the unity of the Spirit, with all who fear God, to have peace with all men what in us lieth, and wherein we err to be instructed by any.

In America, William Brewster was chosen the senior elder of the Pilgrim church. When William Brewster died April 18, 1644, Governor Bradford wrote:

> About the 18th of April died their reverend elder, my dear and loving friend, Mr. William Brewster, a man who had done and suffered much for the Lord Jesus and the Gospel's sake, and had borne his part in the weal or woe with this poor persecuted Church for over thirty-five years in England, Holland, and this wilderness, and had done the Lord and them faithful service in his calling.
>
> Notwithstanding the many troubles and sorrows he passed through, the Lord upheld him to a great age.

Governor Bradford wrote further of elder Brewster:

> He labored in the fields as long as he was able; yet when the church had no other minister he taught twice every Sabbath, and that both powerfully and profitably, to the great edification and comfort of his hearers, many being brought to God by his ministry.

William Brewster is portrayed in the U.S. Capitol Rotunda holding an open Geneva Bible in the painting "Embarkation of the Pilgrims." He is also depicted as representing "religion" in a thematic fresco in the President's room of U.S. Capitol's Senate Wing.

❧

65. PILGRIMS MEET JEWS IN NETHERLANDS

The Dutch country of Holland, also called the Republic of the Seven United Netherlands, experienced a Golden Age from 1568 till Napoleon's conquests in the early 1800s. Holland was one of the few nations not to have a king, though in later years its government operated as limited constitutional monarchy.

Though the Netherlands had adopted the Calvinistic

Protestant Dutch Reformed faith as the State religion, they had a reputation of tolerance which was rare in Europe, extending liberty to other faiths, including Remonstrants, Renaissance Humanism, Catholics, and Anabaptists.

Jews had a history of being persecuted, experiencing a troubled path before finding refuge in Holland.

Spain experienced seven centuries of Islamic occupation, which included episodes of forced conversions and massacres, Ferdinand and Isabella at last drove the last of the Muslims out in 1492. That same year, they sent Columbus on his voyage to find a sea route to India and China.

Under the pretense that some Muslims may be staying in Spain posing as Jews, possibly to attempt a coup or assassinate him, Ferdinand ordered all Jews to convert or leave, thus ending one of the world's largest and most prosperous Sephardic Jewish communities.

Some Jews fled from Spain to the Ottoman Empire, and others fled to Portugal. When the King of Portugal wanted to marry Ferdinand's daughter, he consented on the condition that Portugal institute the same policy of requiring Jews convert or leave.

Recently, in regret of his nation's past policy, the King of Spain, Felipe VI, addressed the Conference of European Rabbis, December 13, 2016:

> Our European identity cannot be understood nor complete without taking into account the decisive contribution of the Jews, who have lived in the continent since the dawn of history ...

> Now—as it did then—Europe needs the invaluable contribution of its Jewish communities, because we need to be honest and respectful to both our common Judeo–Christian values and origins ...

> Esteemed rabbis, I welcome you to Spain,

an open and tolerant country in which respect for diversity is a defining characteristic.

We are also filled with pride by Spain's active and flourishing Jewish community ... (whose) rites, liturgy, renowned surnames, ballads, proverbs and seasonings ... should never have allowed to be lost ...

(In) 1992 ... after entering the Ben Yaacob Synagogue in Madrid, the official welcome was marked by the words of my father King Juan Carlos: "Spanish Jews are in their homeland" ...

Spain's efforts in recent years to return the country's Jewish culture to its rightful state are simply a duty in the name of justice.

The Sephardim's unyielding love and loyalty towards Spain represents a powerful example ... who, for five centuries, stayed true to their heritage.

Many of the Jews who fled from Spain to Portugal soon fled to the Netherlands – Europe's center of religious toleration. They migrated to Holland's largest city of Amsterdam, which in the 1600s became the wealthiest city in the world. Others settled 25 miles away in the city of Leiden.

From its founding by William of Orange in 1575, Leiden University became an intellectual center in Europe. Among its courses were the study of Hebrew, Aramaic and Syriac. A Jewish rabbi reportedly taught in Leiden, as did Pilgrim leader William Brewster.

From the 16th century Renaissance and Reformation to the 17th century Age of Enlightenment, both Protestant and Catholic scholars were captivated with the covenant form of government that existed in the ancient Hebrew Republic, that first 400 year period when Israel came out of Egypt–before they got their first king, Saul.

Scholars were called "Christian Hebraists," as they studied the Hebrew language; the Jewish historian Josephus (37–100 AD); the Jerusalem Talmud (2nd century AD); the Babylonian Talmud (4th century AD); Jewish philosopher Maimonides (1135–1204); and Rabbinic literature. Scholars included:

Thomas Erastus (1524–1583); Bonaventure Vulcanius (1535–1614); Joseph Scaliger (1540–1609); Johannes van den Driesche (1550–1616); Isaac Casaubon (1559–1614); Johannes Buxtorf (1564–1629); Daniel Heinsius (1580–1655); Hugo Grotius (1583–1645); John Selden (1584–1654); Thomas Hobbes (1588–1679); James Harrington (1611–1677); Petrus Cunaeus (1586–1638), who wrote *The Hebrew Republic* in 1617; and John Sadler (1615-1674), whose sister, Ann, married John Harvard, namesake of Harvard University.

Harvard students were required to learn Hebrew, just as Oxford and Cambridge students did in England.

Pilgrims, Puritans, and other Reformed Protestants, identified with the Israelites fleeing from the Egypt, as they too were fleeing persecution. The Pilgrims, numbering around 100, lived in Leiden from 1609 to 1620 before they fled to Massachusetts.

Evidence of the Pilgrims' admiration of Israel was William Bradford statement in *Of Plymouth Plantation*:

> Though I am grown aged, yet I have had a longing desire, to see with my own eyes, something of the most ancient language, and holy tongue, in which the Law, and oracles of God were writ; and in which God, and angels, spoke to the holy patriarchs, of old time; and what names were given to things, from the creation.
>
> And though I cannot attain to much herein, yet I am refreshed, to have seen some glimpse hereof; (as Moses say the Land of Canaan afar

off) my aim and desire is, to see how the words, and phrases lye in the holy text; and to discern somewhat of the same for my own content.

Indeed, a Hebrew phrase is included in the inscription on Governor William Bradford's grave at Burial Hill in Plymouth, Massachusetts:

> Under this stone rests the ashes of William Bradford, a zealous Puritan, and sincere Christian Governor of Plymouth Colony from 1621 to 1657, aged 69, except 5 years, which he declined. [Hebrew phrase] *"Let the right hand of the Lord awake."* [Latin phrase] *"What our fathers with so much difficulty attained do not basely relinquish."*

In Leiden, the Pilgrims would have become acquainted with Jewish Thanksgiving feast of Tabernacles or "Sukkot," which was celebrated annually September–October.

Also in Leiden, an annual day of thanksgiving was celebrated each October in remembrance of the ending of the bloody "Spanish Furies" committed by Spain's "Iron Duke" from 1572–1576.

<5

66. PILGRIMS CONSIDERED GUIANA

After 12 years in Holland, the Pilgrims began to see their children assimilating into the Dutch culture. Realizing their courageous separatist movement may be short-lived, and facing the looming threat of Spain again invading Holland, the Pilgrims became convinced they had to leave.

Some proposed sailing to Dutch Guiana in South America, possibly to Essequibo, as they heard of its tropical climate. This was decided against this when they remembered how the Spanish Governor Menéndez annihilated the French Protestant Huguenots of Fort Caroline in 1565.

Governor Bradford wrote in *Of Plymouth Plantation*:

> Some ... had thoughts and were earnest for
> Guiana ... Those for Guiana alleged that the
> country was rich, fruitful, and blessed with a
> perpetual spring ... but to this it was answered,
> that it was out of question ...

> If they should there live, and do well, the
> jealous Spaniard would never suffer them long,
> but would displant or overthrow them, as he
> did the French in Florida.

❧

67. PILGRIMS–ALMOST DUTCH SETTLERS

In 1609, the Dutch East India Company employed English explorer Henry Hudson to find a Northwest Passage sea route to India and China. He explored Canada and the area of New York, with the Hudson River being named for him.

Unfortunately for him, in 1611, Hudson's crew mutinied and put him, his son, and seven companions, in a small boat and sent them adrift. They were never seen again.

In 1614, the Dutch established Fort Nassau as a fur trading post along the Hudson River. Dutch companies approached the Pilgrims in an attempt to persuade them to settle in Dutch controlled territory, but the Pilgrims declined, opting to join England's Virginia Colony.

In 1621, the Dutch West India Company was chartered, and in 1624, it sent over settlers to replace Fort Nassau with a new fort on higher ground two miles to the north named Fort Orange. This is considered the first permanent Dutch settlement in North America, growing into the city of Albany.

These forts were named for Maurice, Prince of Orange and Nassau, who was elected "stadtholder" of the Dutch Republic from 1585 to 1625, following the death in 1584 of his father, William the Silent.

In 1624, the Dutch settled Governor's Island, just 800 yards from Manhattan Island. In 1625, they settled the city of New Amsterdam. Staten Island was named for the Dutch Parliament, which is called "Staten-Generaal."

∿

68. PILGRIMS DEPART FROM HOLLAND

The Pilgrims left Delfts-Haven, Holland, for England on July 22, 1620, on the *Speedwell*, with the blessings of their separatist pastor, John Robinson.

William Bradford described their departure:

> So being ready to depart, they had a day of solemn humiliation, their pastor taking his text from Ezra 8:21:
>
> "And there at ye river, by Ahava, I proclaimed a fast, that we might humble ourselves before our God and seek of Him a right way for us, and for our Children, and for our substance" ...
>
> The rest of the time was spent in powering out prayers to ye Lord with great fervency, mixed with abundance of tears.
>
> And ye time being come that they must depart, they were accompanied with most of their brethren out of ye city, unto a town sundry miles off called Delfts-Haven, where the ship lay ready to receive them.
>
> So they left ye goodly and pleasant city, which had been there resting place for near 12 years; but they knew they were pilgrims (Hebrews 12), but lift their eyes to ye heavens, their dearest country, and quieted their spirits.

Senator Robert Byrd told Congress, June 27, 1962:

> Inside the rotunda is a picture of the Pilgrims about to embark from Holland on the sister ship of the *Mayflower*, the *Speedwell*.

The ship's revered chaplain, Brewster, who later joined the *Mayflower*, has open on his lap the Bible. Very clear are the words, "the New Testament according to our Lord and Savior, Jesus Christ." On the sail is the motto of the Pilgrims, "God With Us."

∽

69. PILGRIMS DEPART FROM ENGLAND

On August 5, 1620, they left England on their first attempt for America, aboard the *Speedwell* and the *Mayflower*. The *Speedwell* leaked, so they returned to Dartmouth, England for repairs.

They made a second attempt on August 21, 1620, but after 300 miles, the *Speedwell* leaked again. When they returned, the *Speedwell* was deemed unusable, and 11 of its passengers boarded the *Mayflower*.

On September 6, 1620, carrying 102 passengers (73 males and 29 females) the 90-foot-long *Mayflower* departed on its 66–day journey of 2,750 miles.

They encountered storms so rough that the beam supporting the main mast cracked. It was propped back in place with "a great iron screw," which they had brought along for help with house construction.

One youth, John Howland, was swept overboard by a freezing wave and rescued. His descendants include Ralph Waldo Emerson, Humphrey Bogart, Franklin D. Roosevelt and George W. Bush. During the Pilgrims' voyage, one crew member and one passenger died and a mother gave birth to a child named Oceanus.

They were intending to land in Virginia and join the Jamestown Colony, where the king–appointed Governor was Sir George Yeardley.

The stormy weather, though, had blown the *Mayflower* 500 miles off–course. When they finally sighted land on November 9, 1620, William Brewster led them in a prayer of thanksgiving from Psalm 100.

Of their safe arrival, William Bradford wrote:

> Being thus arrived in a good harbor, and
> brought safe to land, they fell upon their
> knees and blessed the God of Heaven who
> had brought them over the vast and furious
> ocean, and delivered them from all the perils
> and miseries thereof, again to set their feet on
> the firm and stable earth, their proper element.

The captain, Christopher Jones, attempted to go back to sea and sail south towards the Hudson River then to Virginia, but the ship almost sank in high winds and treacherous currents near shoals off Cape Cod. The dangerous area is known as an "ocean graveyard."

Returning to anchor at Provincetown, November 11, 1620, ship master Christopher Jones informed the Pilgrims that they had to disembark and begin their settlement here – but this caused a government crisis.

⌁

70. THREE TYPES OF COLONIES

There were three types of colonies:

1) COMPANY CHARTER COLONY – created with the permission of the king, having investors and company bylaws. The Virginia Company was given a charter in 1606. After experiencing disease, starvation and a massacre in 1622, the Company went bankrupt and the King appointed a governor in 1624.

2) ROYAL CROWN COLONY – ruled directly by the King through his appointed governor, but in most cases the King provided no financial support.

In Virginia's case, the governors demanded landowners provide his funding, but left it up to them to determine how. The landowners elected a leader from each district, called a burgess. The burgesses met to decide how much each would pay to the governor, but then they began to make decision on other issues.

This birthed a degree of autonomy in the Virginia House of Burgesses – the first legislative assembly in the New World.

3) PROPRIETARY COLONY – where land was given by the king to a private individual, such as:

•Maryland was originally granted by King Charles I as private property to Lord Baltimore in 1632, as a haven for persecuted Catholics;

•The Carolinas were originally given by King Charles II as private property to seven lord proprietors in 1663;

•New York was originally given by King Charles II as private property to his younger brother, the Duke of York, in 1664;

•Pennsylvania was given by King Charles II as private property to William Penn in 1681.

Each of these three types of colonies operated under the King's authority.

The Pilgrims had intended on sailing to the Jamestown Colony and submit to the king–appointed government, but when storms caused them to land in Massachusetts, they faced a dilemma – there was no king–appointed person on board to take charge.

To solve this, the Pilgrims did something unprecedented – they gave themselves the authority and created their own government – the *Mayflower Compact*, signed November 11, 1620.

This was the beginning of a polarity change in world government. Instead of a top–down government being ruled by the will of a king, this was an experiment in a bottom–up form of government, being ruled by the will of the people. The *Mayflower Compact* began:

In ye name of God, Amen. We whose names are underwritten, the loyall subjects

of our dread soveraigne Lord, King James ...
having undertaken, for ye glorie of God, and
advancemente of ye Christian faith, and honour
of our king & countrie, a voyage to plant ye
first colonie in ye Northerne parts of Virginia ...

In ye presence of God, and one of another,
covenant & combine our selves togeather into a
civill body politick ... to enacte ... just & equall
lawes ... as shall be thought most meete &
convenient for ye generall good of ye Colonie,
unto which we promise all due submission &
obedience ...

In witnes wherof we have hereunder
subscribed our names at Cap–Codd ye 11 of
NOVEMBER, Ano:Dom. 1620.

Pilgrims chose John Carver as their first governor.

✌

71. IDEA OF SELF-GOVERNMENT

Where did the Pilgrims get the idea for self-
government contained in the *Mayflower Compact*?

From their separatist Pastor John Robinson, who is
considered one of the founders of the Congregational
Church. Pastor Robinson addressed the Pilgrims aboard
the *Speedwell,* July 22, 1620, as they prepared to depart
from Holland's Delfts-Haven harbor:

Lastly, whereas you are become a body
politic, using amongst yourselves civil
government, let your wisdom and godliness
appear not only in choosing such persons
as do entirely love and will promote the
common good, but also in yielding unto
them all due honor and obedience in their
lawful administrations; not beholding in them
the ordinariness of their persons, but God's
ordinance for your good ....

Someone or few must needs be appointed
over the assembly ... discussing and determining

of all matters, so in this royal assembly, the church of Christ, though all be Kings, yet some most faithful and most able, are to be set over the rest ... wherein ... they are ... charged to minister according to the Testament of Christ.

For I am very confident the Lord hath more truth and light yet to break forth out of His Holy Word.

Earlier, Pastor John Robinson and William Brewster wrote from Leiden to London financier Sir Edwin Sandys, December 15, 1617, explaining the Pilgrims were:

Knit together as a body in most strict and sacred bond and covenant of the lord, of the violation whereof we make great conscience, and by virtue whereof we so hold ourselves straitly tied to all care of each other's good, and of the whole by everyone and so mutually.

"Compact" referred to people in "commonwealth" or "covenant" under God – a concept studied in great depth by Reformation scholars, such as: John Calvin, Huldrych Zwingli, John Knox, and Thomas Cromwell.

Pastor Robinson is prominently depicted kneeling in prayer next to elder William Brewster, who is holding an open Bible, in the painting *The Embarkation of the Pilgrims*, which hangs in the U.S. Capitol Rotunda.

An insight into the Pilgrims' faith is seen in a letter Pastor Robinson wrote from Leiden:

Thus this holy army of saints is marshaled here on earth by these officers, under the conduct of their glorious Emperor, Christ.

Thus it marches in this most heavenly order and gracious array, against all enemies, both bodily and ghostly: peaceable in itself, as Jerusalem, terrible to the enemy as an army with banners, triumphing over their tyranny with patience, their cruelty with meekness, and over death itself with dying.

Thus, through the Blood of that spotless Lamb, and that Word of their testimony, they are more than conquerors, bruising the head of the Serpent; yea, through the power of His Word, they have power to cast down Satan like lightning; to tread upon serpents and scorpions; to cast down strongholds, and everything that exalteth itself against God.

The gates of hell, and all the principalities and powers on earth shall not prevail against it.

∽

72. CHANGE IN DIRECTION OF POWER

At the time of America's founding, nearly the entire world was ruled by kings who claimed to have a "divine right" to rule over people. The question the settlers wrestled with was:

does POWER flow from the Creator—to the King—to the People; or does POWER flow from the Creator—to the People—to their Political Leaders?

In 1629, William Brewster commented on their self-government:

The church that had been brought over the ocean now saw another church, the first–born in America, holding the same faith in the same simplicity of self-government under Christ alone.

"Covenant" theology was held by persecuted Puritans who began arriving ten years after the Pilgrims. Puritan leader John Winthrop wrote in *A Model of Christian Charity*, June 11, 1630:

We are a Company, professing ourselves fellow members of Christ, we ought to account ourselves knit together by this bond of love ... by a mutual consent through a special over ruling Providence ... to seek out a place of Cohabitation ...

Thus stands the cause between God and us: we are entered into covenant with Him for this work ... The Lord hath given us leave to draw our own articles ... For this end, we must be knit together in this work as one man ...

We must ... make one another's condition our own, rejoice together, mourn together, labor and suffer together, always having before our eyes our Commission and Community in this work, as members of the same body.

So shall we keep the unity of the Spirit in the bond of peace ... We shall find that the God of Israel is among us ... We shall be as a City upon a Hill, the eyes of all people are upon us.

John D. Eusden wrote in *Natural Law and Covenant Theology in New England, 1620–1670* (Notre Dame Law School, *Natural Law Forum*. 1960, Paper 47):

The idea of the covenant – that central, permeating idea of Puritanism ... Covenanted men actually constructed political communities – the emerging "American character" in the realm of governmental theory and jurisprudence ...

Names dominate the dramatis personae:

•John Cotton, influential minister of the First Church in Boston ...

•John Winthrop, long–time governor of the Massachusetts Bay Colony ...

•Nathaniel Ward, chief framer of the 1641 Body of Liberties for the Bay Colony;

•William Bradford, governor of Plymouth Plantation;

•Thomas Hooker, preacher and potentate of Hartford;

•John Norton, official apologist for New England Congregationalism;

•John Eliot, evangelist and occasional

political writer; and

• John Davenport, founder of New Haven ...

Political and social thought of early American Puritanism was drawn from four sources: the Bible, the covenant tradition in Reformation theology, the common law of England, and the long Western tradition of natural law.

Puritans back in England attempted to have a covenant government, called "Commonwealth," in 1649, led by Lord Protector Oliver Cromwell. In 1657, Oliver Cromwell allowed Jews back into England, ending the banishment enacted by Edward I in 1290.

After Cromwell died, a royalist movement restored monarchy to England by putting King Charles II on the throne. Os Guinness stated in an interview on "Thinking in Public" with Dr. Albert Mohler, June 5, 2017:

> The covenantal ideas in England were the lost cause, sadly. They failed. The king came back. But the lost cause became the winning cause in New England. And covenant shaped constitutionalism ...
>
> The American Constitution is a nationalized, secularized form of covenant ... Covenant lies behind constitution.

To perpetuate appreciation for the Pilgrims, the Plymouth Rock Foundation was founded in 1970:

> To make more widely known and understood the Pilgrim principles and characteristics – their devotion to God and the Bible, to freedom and to tolerance, and their embodiment of courage, brotherhood, and individual moral character.

Dr. Paul Jehle, Executive Director of the Plymouth Rock Foundation, whose ancestors were on the *Mayflower*, wrote "*Mayflower Compact* Day" (Plymouth Rock Foundation's E–News, November, 2011):

We remember when the *Mayflower Compact* was signed on board the *Mayflower*, while it lay anchored in what is now Provincetown Harbor, November 11, 1620 ...

A compact is a covenant ... Since the Pilgrims were children of the Reformation, their view of covenant came from the Bible ...

Dr. Jehle continued:

It was God that initiated the concept of covenant, first with Adam and Eve (Genesis 2:15–17 and 2:24). God also made a covenant with Noah in Genesis 9 and of course the process of 'cutting' covenant was depicted in visual form for Abraham in Genesis 15.

Throughout the Bible covenants were used both vertically (with God directly) and horizontally (with humans) to depict God's process of bringing people into unity with Him and one another. Unity of purpose and harmony with God set the highest ideals for good behavior.

Dr. Jehle added:

No wonder when Pastor John Robinson sent his farewell letter to the Pilgrims upon their departure in 1620, knowing that they would need to form their own civil government, he gave this sound advice:

"Whereas you are become a body politic, using amongst yourselves civil government, and are not furnished with any persons of special eminency above the rest, to be chosen by you into office of government;

let your wisdom and godliness appear, not only in choosing such persons as do entirely love and will promote the common good ... not being like the foolish multitude who more honor the gay coat than either the virtuous mind of the man, or glorious ordinance of the Lord."

73. SQUANTO

Of 102 Pilgrims that landed in Massachusetts in November of 1620, only half survived the harsh winter.

William Bradford wrote:

> What could now sustain them but ye spirit of God and His grace? ...
>
> Ought not the children of these fathers rightly say: Our fathers ... came over this great ocean, and were ready to perish in this wilderness; but they cried unto ye Lord, and He heard their voice.

To provide for the colony's defense, the Pilgrims originally approached Captain John Smith but then decided to hire Captain Miles Standish. Standish led them in exploring the new territory, directed the building of barricades, and defended against hostile attacks.

American poet Henry Wadsworth Longfellow wrote the classic narrative poem, *The Courtship of Miles Standish*, 1858, which sold 10,000 copies in London in a single day.

In 1621, after Pilgrim Governor John Carver died, William Bradford was chosen governor, being reelected 30 times till his death.

Bradford was born March 19, 1590, two years after Spain attempted to invade England with its Armada. At age 17, the same year Shakespeare produced his play, *Anthony and Cleopatra,* Bradford fled from England to Holland with the persecuted Pilgrims.

At age 30, he left Holland and sailed with the Pilgrims to America. Bradford's journal, *Of Plymouth Plantation*, was the main historical record of the Pilgrims, being published in 1650. In the Spring of 1621, he recorded in *Of Plymouth Plantation*:

About the 16th of March, a certain Indian came boldly amongst them and spoke to them in broken English ... His name was Samoset.

He told them also of another Indian whose name was Squanto, a native of this place, who had been in England and could speak better English than himself ...

Massasoyt, who about four or five days after, came with the chief of his friends and other attendants, and with Squanto.

With him, after friendly entertainment and some gifts, they made a peace which has now continued for twenty-four years.

Samoset's initial visit to the Pilgrims was recorded in *Mourt's Relation*, 1622:

Friday the 16th a fair warm day towards; this morning we determined to conclude of the military orders, which we had begun to consider of before but were interrupted by the savages, as we mentioned formerly; and whilst we were busied hereabout, we were interrupted again, for there presented himself a savage, which caused an alarm.

He very boldly came all alone and along the houses straight to the rendezvous, where we intercepted him, not suffering him to go in, as undoubtedly he would, out of his boldness.

He saluted us in English, and bade us welcome, for he had learned some broken English among the Englishmen that came to fish at Monchiggon, and knew by name the most of the captains, commanders, and masters that usually come.

He was a man free in speech, so far as he could express his mind, and of a seemly carriage. We questioned him of many things; he was the first savage we could meet withal.

He said he was not of these parts, but of Morattiggon, and one of the sagamores or lords thereof, and had been eight months in these parts, it lying hence a day's sail with a great wind, and five days by land.

He discoursed of the whole country, and of every province, and of their sagamores, and their number of men, and strength.

The wind being to rise a little, we cast a horseman's coat about him, for he was stark naked, only a leather about his waist, with a fringe about a span long, or little more; he had a bow and two arrows, the one headed, and the other unheaded.

He was a tall straight man, the hair of his head black, long behind, only short before, none on his face at all; he asked some beer, but we gave him strong water and biscuit, and butter, and cheese, and pudding, and a piece of mallard, all which he liked well, and had been acquainted with such amongst the English.

He told us the place where we now live is called Patuxet, and that about four years ago all the inhabitants died of an extraordinary plague, and there is neither man, woman, nor child remaining, as indeed we have found none, so as there is none to hinder our possession, or to lay claim unto it.

All the afternoon we spent in communication with him; we would gladly have been rid of him at night, but he was not willing to go this night.

Then we thought to carry him on shipboard, wherewith he was well content, and went into the shallop, but the wind was high and the water scant, that it could not return back. We lodged him that night at Stephen Hopkins' house, and watched him.

The next day he went away back to the

Massasoits, from whence he said he came, who are our next bordering neighbors. They are sixty strong, as he saith.

The Nausets are as near southeast of them, and are a hundred strong, and those were they of whom our people were encountered, as before related.

They are much incensed and provoked against the English, and about eight months ago slew three Englishmen, and two more hardly escaped by flight to Monchiggon; they were Sir Ferdinando Gorges his men, as this savage told us, as he did likewise of the huggery, that is, fight, that our discoverers had with the Nausets, and of our tools that were taken out of the woods, which we willed him should be brought again, otherwise, we would right ourselves.

These people are ill affected towards the English, by reason of one Hunt, a master of a ship, who deceived the people, and got them under color of trucking with them, twenty out of this very place where we inhabit, and seven men from Nauset, and carried them away, and sold them for slaves like a wretched man (for twenty pound a man) that cares not what mischief he doth for his profit.

Saturday, in the morning we dismissed the savage, and gave him a knife, a bracelet, and a ring; he promised within a night or two to come again, and to bring with him some of the Massasoits, our neighbors, with such beavers' skins as they had to truck with us.

Though records are scarce, it appears Squanto was kidnapped around 1605, with other Patuxet natives, by George Weymouth's expedition. Taken to England, he lived with Sir Ferdinando Gorges of Plymouth.

In 1614, Sir Ferdinando Gorges made another

expedition to New England for the purpose of mapping the coast. Squanto accompanied him as interpreter.

Allowed to return to his tribe, Squanto, with other Patuxet and Nausets natives, were kidnapped by Captain Thomas Hunt, who intended to sell them in the slave markets of Malaga, a city notorious for the slave trade dating back to the Muslim occupation of Spain.

Governor Bradford wrote of Squanto:

> He was a native of these parts, and had been one of the few survivors of the plague hereabouts. He was carried away with others by one Hunt, a captain of a ship, who intended to sell them for slaves in Spain.

Squanto was rescued by some Christian friars, who introduced him to Christianity and gave him his freedom. He returned to England where he was hired by John Slaney, treasurer of the Newfoundland Company. He then worked for John Mason, Governor of the Newfoundland Colony, and following that, for Captain Thomas Dermer, agent of Sir Ferdinando Gorges. Governor Bradford wrote of Squanto:

> He got away for England, and was received by a merchant in London, and employed in Newfoundland and other parts, and lastly brought into these parts by a Captain Dermer, a gentleman employed by Sir Ferdinand Gorges.

When Squanto finally returned in 1619, he found that his entire tribe had died in a plague. Depressed, he lived with the neighboring Wampanoag tribe. As tragic as his kidnapping was, had he not been kidnapped, Squanto most likely would have died in that plague.

Pilgrim Governor William Bradford continued:

> Captain Dermer had been here the same year that the people of the *Mayflower* arrived, as appears in an account written by him, and given to me by a friend, bearing date, June 30th, 1620...

"I will first begin," says he, "with the place from which Squanto (or Tisquantem) was taken away, which in Captain Smith's map is called Plymouth; and I would that Plymouth (England) had the same commodities.

I could wish that the first plantation might be situated here, if there came to the number of fifty persons or upward; otherwise at Charlton, because there the savages are less to be feared ...

The Pokanokets (Patuxet), who live to the west of Plymouth, bear an inveterate hatred to the English ... For this reason Squanto cannot deny but they would have killed me when I was at Namasket, had he not interceded hard for me."

The plague that wiped out the Patuxet may have come from survivors of a French shipwreck at Cape Code in 1617, three years before the Pilgrims landed. Bradford described:

About three years before, a French ship was wrecked at Cape Cod, but the men got ashore and saved their lives and a large part of their provisions.

When the Indians heard of it, they surrounded them and never left watching and dogging them till they got the advantage and killed them, all but three or four, whom they kept, and sent from one Sachem to another, making sport with them and using them worse than slaves.

Dutch historian Jeremy Dupertuis Bangs noted that from a European sailor's grave the Pilgrims later removed some objects, but avoided disturbing what they recognized as Indian graves. Edward Winslow reported that upon discovering "a bow with rotted arrows" in a mound:

We supposed there were many other things, but because we deemed them graves, we put in the bow again and made it up as it was, and left the rest untouched, because we thought it would be odious unto them to ransack their sepulchres.

Squanto put the Pilgrims on good terms with the Wampanoag tribe. Governor Bradford described Squanto as "a special instrument sent of God," writing:

Squanto stayed with them and was their interpreter and was a special instrument sent of God for their good beyond their expectation. He showed them how to plant corn, where to take fish and other commodities, and guided them to unknown places, and never left them till he died.

❦

74. PILGRIMS' FIRST THANKSGIVING

Governor Bradford added how the next year, with the help of Squanto, the Pilgrims had an abundant harvest in 1621.

The settlers, as many as were able, then began to plant their corn, in which service Squanto stood them in good stead, showing them how to plant it and cultivate it.

He also told them that unless they got fish to manure this exhausted old soil, it would come to nothing, and he showed them that in the middle of April plenty of fish would come up the brook by which they had begun to build, and taught them how to catch it, and where to get other necessary provisions; all of which they found true by experience.

Pilgrim leader Edward Winslow wrote in *Mourt's Relation*:

Our harvest being gotten in, our governor sent four men on fowling, that so we might after a special manner rejoice together after we had gathered the fruit of our labors.

They four in one day killed as much fowl as, with a little help beside, served the company almost a week.

At which time, amongst other recreations, we exercised our arms, many of the Indians coming amongst us, and among the rest their greatest king Massasoit, with some ninety men, whom for three days we entertained and feasted, and they went out and killed five deer, which they brought to the plantation and bestowed on our Governor, and upon the Captain and others.

And although it be not always so plentiful, as it was at this time, with us, yet by goodness of God, we are so far from want, that we often wish you partakers of our plenty.

Bradford described the autumn of 1621:

And besides waterfowl there was great store of wild turkeys, of which they took many, besides venison, etc. Besides, they had about a peck a meal a week to a person, or now since harvest, Indian corn to that proportion.

Ben Franklin wrote of the Pilgrims' Thanksgiving (*The Compleated Autobiography by Benjamin Franklin,* editors Mark & Jo Ann Skousen, Regnery, 2006, p. 331):

There is a tradition that in the planting of New England, the first settlers met with many difficulties and hardships, as is generally the case when a civiliz'd people attempt to establish themselves in a wilderness country.

Being so piously dispos'd, they sought relief from heaven by laying their wants and distresses before the Lord in frequent set days of fasting and prayer.

Constant meditation and discourse on these subjects kept their minds gloomy and discontented, and like the children of Israel there were many dispos'd to return to the Egypt which persecution had induc'd them to abandon ...

Franklin continued:

> At length, when it was proposed in the Assembly to proclaim another fast, a farmer of plain sense rose and remark'd that the inconveniences they suffer'd, and concerning which they had so often weary'd heaven with their complaints, were not so great as they might have expected, and were diminishing every day as the colony strengthen'd;

> that the earth began to reward their labour and furnish liberally for their subsistence; that their seas and rivers were full of fish, the air sweet, the climate healthy, and above all, they were in the full enjoyment of liberty, civil and religious.

> He therefore thought that reflecting and conversing on these subjects would be more comfortable and lead more to make them contented with their situation; and that it would be more becoming the gratitude they ow'd to the divine being, if instead of a fast they should proclaim a thanksgiving.

> His advice was taken, and from that day to this, they have in every year observ'd circumstances of public felicity sufficient to furnish employment for a Thanksgiving Day, which is therefore constantly ordered and religiously observed.

The Pilgrims' Thanksgiving traditions were documented by Dutch historian, Jeremy Dupertuis Bangs (Ph.D. Leiden, 1976), who wrote: *Church Art and Architecture in the Low Countries before 1566* (1997); *The Seventeenth-Century Town Records of Scituate, Massachusetts* (3 vols., 1997, 1999, 2001); *Indian Deeds, Land Transactions in Plymouth Colony, 1620-1699* (2002); and *Pilgrim Edward Winslow, New England's First International Diplomat* (2004).

Bangs authored articles about the Dutch "Remonstrants" and the "Pilgrim Fathers" in the *Routledge Encyclopedia of Protestantism* (Hans Hillerbrand, ed.), and had articles published in *The Mayflower Quarterly*. Jeremy Dupertuis Bangs wrote:

> Our knowledge of the 1621 Thanksgiving comes from Winslow and Bradford. Winslow's choice of words, understood by his contemporaries, implies to us that the Pilgrims gave thanks to God for their preservation and for the plenty that gave hope for the future.
>
> Winslow specifically tells us that the colonists sat down with their Native neighbors and enjoyed several days of peaceful rejoicing together. It is a history with potent symbolism, and it needs neither apology nor distortion.

Bangs added:

> When Winslow described the Pilgrims' intention, "after a more special manner [to] rejoice together, after we had gathered the fruit of our labors," he was alluding to John 4: 36 and to Psalm 33.
>
> The first is, "And he that reapeth, receiveth wages, & gathereth fruit unto life eternal, that both he that soweth, & he that reapeth, might rejoice together."

Two years after the Pilgrim landing, there was a drought in 1623, Governor Bradford wrote:

> And afterwards the Lord sent them such seasonable showers, with interchange of fair warm weather as, through His blessing, caused a fruitful and liberal harvest, to their no small comfort and rejoicing.
>
> For which mercy, in time convenient, they also set apart a day of thanksgiving.
>
> By this time harvest was come, and instead of famine now God gave them plenty - for

which they blessed God.

And the effect of their particular planting was well seen, for all had - pretty well - so as any general want or famine had not been amongst them since to this day.

Decades later, a thanksgiving proclamation was issued by the Governing Council of Charlestown, Massachusetts, June 20, 1676:

The Council has thought meet to appoint ... a day of solemn Thanksgiving and praise to God ... that the Lord may behold us as a people offering praise and thereby glorifying Him;

the Council doth commend it to the respective ministers, elders and people of this jurisdiction; solemnly and seriously to keep the same beseeching that being persuaded by the mercies of God we may all, even this whole people offer up our bodies and souls as a living and acceptable Service unto God by Jesus Christ.

Franklin Roosevelt stated in his Thanksgiving Day Proclamation, October 31, 1939:

More than three centuries ago at the season of the gathering in of the harvest, the Pilgrims humbly paused in their work and gave thanks to God for the preservation of their community and for the abundant yield of the soil.

The U.S. Congress, approved a joint resolution December 26, 1941, designating the fourth Thursday in November of each year as National Thanksgiving Day.

Congress passed a Joint Resolution, April 17, 1952, to set aside an annual National Day of Prayer:

From its beginning the United States of America has been a nation fully cognizant of the value of prayer. In the early days of colonization, the Pilgrims frequently engaged in prayer.

President John F. Kennedy proclaimed a National Thanksgiving Day, October 28, 1961:

More than three centuries ago, the Pilgrims, after a year of hardship and peril, humbly and reverently set aside a special day upon which to give thanks to God for their preservation and for the good harvest from the virgin soil upon which they had labored. Grave and unknown dangers remained.

Yet by their faith and by their toil they had survived the rigors of the harsh New England winter. Hence they paused in their labors to give thanks for the blessings that had been bestowed upon them by Divine Providence.

We give thanks ... for the heritage of liberty bequeathed by our ancestors which we are privileged to preserve for our children and our children's children ...

I ask the head of each family to recount to his children the story of the first New England Thanksgiving, thus to impress upon future generations the heritage of this nation born in toil, in danger, in purpose, and in the conviction that right and justice and freedom can through man's efforts persevere and come to fruition with the blessing of God.

Kennedy proclaimed November 7, 1962:

Over three centuries ago in Plymouth, on Massachusetts Bay, the Pilgrims established the custom of gathering together each year to express their gratitude to God for the preservation of their community and for the harvests their labors brought forth in the new land.

Joining with their neighbors, they shared together and worshiped together in a common giving of thanks ...

We recognize that we are the beneficiaries

of the toil and devotion of our fathers and that we can pass their legacy on to our children ...

Let us renew the spirit of the Pilgrims at the first Thanksgiving, lonely in an inscrutable wilderness, facing the dark unknown with a faith borne of their dedication to God and a fortitude drawn from their sense that all men were brothers.

Kennedy stated in his Thanksgiving Proclamation, November 5, 1963:

Over three centuries ago, our forefathers in Virginia and in Massachusetts, far from home in a lonely wilderness, set aside a time of thanksgiving.

On the appointed day, they gave reverent thanks for their safety, for the health of their children, for the fertility of their fields, for the love which bound them together and for the faith which united them with their God.

President Donald J. Trump stated in his Thanksgiving Proclamation, November 23, 2017:

In July 1620, more than 100 Pilgrims boarded the Mayflower, fleeing religious persecution and seeking freedom and opportunity in a new and unfamiliar place. These dauntless souls arrived in Plymouth, Massachusetts, in the freezing cold of December 1620. They were greeted by sickness and severe weather, and quickly lost 46 of their fellow travelers.

Those who endured the incredible hardship of their first year in America, however, had many reasons for gratitude ...

In thanks to God for these blessings, the new governor of the Plymouth Colony, William Bradford, proclaimed a day of thanksgiving and gathered with the Wampanoag tribe for three days of celebration ...

I encourage all Americans to gather, in homes and places of worship, to offer a prayer of thanks to God for our many blessings.

❧

75. PILGRIMS' DAY OF FASTING

A second boatload of Pilgrims arrived on November 9, 1621, on the ship *Fortune*. Unfortunately, they did not bring supplies, resulting in the second winter being a starving time.

The Pilgrims filled the *Fortune* with £500 worth of valuable furs and goods to start paying back their debt to the investors, called "merchant adventurers," who financed their trip.

Three weeks later, the ship set sail back to England. Tragically, it was captured by the French and all the supplies stolen, leaving the Pilgrims in greater deficit.

Edward Winslow recorded the Pilgrims' response to tragedy, reprinted in *Alexander Young's Chronicles of the Pilgrims* (Boston, 1841), stated:

> Drought and the like considerations moved not only every good man privately to enter into examination with his own estate between God and his conscience, and so to humiliation before Him, but also to humble ourselves together before the Lord by Fasting and Prayer.

❧

76. SQUANTO'S DEATH WAS A GREAT LOSS

Bradford wrote of an incident involving Squanto:

> Another Indian, called Hobbamok came to live with them, a fine strong man, of some account amongst the Indians for his valor and qualities. He remained very faithful to the English till he died.
>
> He and Squanto having gone upon business among the Indians, a Sachem called Corbitant

... began to quarrel with them, and threatened to stab Hobbamok; but he being a strong man, cleared himself of him, and came running away, all sweating, and told the Governor what had befallen him, and that he feared they had killed Squanto ...

So it was resolved to send the Captain and fourteen men, well armed ... The Captain, giving orders to let none escape, entered to search for him.

But Corbitant had gone away that day; so they missed him, but learned that Squanto was alive, and that Corbitant had only threatened to kill him, and made as if to stab him, but did not ...

Bradford told of Squanto's death in September 1622:

After this, on the 18th of September, they sent out their shallop (small sailboat) with ten men and Squanto as guide and interpreter to the Massachusetts, to explore the bay and trade with the natives, which they accomplished, and were kindly received ...

Nor was there a man among them who had ever seen a beaver skin till they came out, and were instructed by Squanto ...

Captain Standish was appointed to go with them, and Squanto as a guide and interpreter, about the latter end of September; but the winds drove them in; and putting out again, Captain Standish fell ill with fever, so the Governor (Bradford) went himself.

But they could not get round the shoals of Cape Cod, for flats and breakers, and Squanto could not direct them better.

The Captain of the boat dare not venture any further, so they put into Manamoick Bay, and got what they could there ...

Bradford concluded:

> Here Squanto fell ill of Indian fever,
> bleeding much at the nose, which the Indians
> take for a symptom of death, and within a few
> days he died.

> He begged the Governor to pray for him,
> that he might go to the Englishmen's God in
> Heaven, and bequeathed several of his things to
> some of his English friends, as remembrances.
> His death was a great loss.

∽

77. PILGRIMS TRIED COMMUNISM

The merchant adventurers set up the "Plymouth
Plantation" as a "company" colony, having obtained
a land patent from the Virginia Company of London.

The company bylaws were structured so that the
merchant adventurers would make a profit on the
colony. The bylaws required Pilgrims "planters" live in
a communal system for the first seven years, in which
all capital and profits remained "in ye common stock":

> The adventurers & planters do agree that
> every person that goeth being aged 16 years &
> upward ... be accounted a single share ...

> The persons transported & ye adventurers
> shall continue their joint stock & partnership
> together, ye space of 7 years ... during which
> time, all profits & benefits that are got by trade,
> traffic, trucking, working, fishing, or any other
> means of any person or persons, remain still in
> ye common stock ...

> That all such persons as are of this colony,
> are to have their meat, drink, apparel, and all
> provision out of ye common stock & goods ...

> That at ye end of ye 7 years, ye capital
> & profits, viz. the houses, lands, goods

and chattels, be equally divided betwixt ye adventurers, and planters.

Governor Bradford described in *Of Plymouth Plantation* that the sharing of "all profits & benefits ... in ye common stock," regardless of how hard each individual worked, was a failure:

> The failure of that experiment of communal service, which was tried for several years, and by good and honest men, proves the emptiness of the theory of Plato and other ancients, applauded by some of later times,–

> that the taking away of private property, and the possession of it in community, by a commonwealth, would make a state happy and flourishing; as it they were wiser than God ...

> For in this instance, community of property was found to breed much confusion and discontent; and retard much employment which would have been to the general benefit ...

> For the young men who were most able and fit for service objected to being forced to spend their time and strength in working for other men's wives and children, without any recompense ...

Bradford continued:

> The strong man or the resourceful man had no more share of food, clothes, etc., than the weak man who was not able to do a quarter the other could.

> This was thought injustice. The aged and graver men, who were ranked and equalized in labor, food, clothes, etc., with the humbler and younger ones, thought it some indignity and disrespect to them.

> As for men's wives who were obliged to do service for other men, such as cooking, washing their clothes, etc., they considered it

a kind of slavery, and many husbands would not brook it ...

Bradford explained that the "communistic plan" of redistributing wealth failed:

> If all were to share alike, and all were to do alike, then all were on an equality throughout, and one was as good as another; and so, if it did not actually abolish those very relations which God himself has set among men, it did at least greatly diminish the mutual respect that is so important should be preserved amongst them.

> Let none argue that this is due to human failing, rather than to this communistic plan of life in itself.

In 1626, Captain Miles Standish was sent back to England to negotiate with Isaac Allerton and the leading men of Plymouth to pay off the colony's debt to the Adventurers. This was successful in freeing Pilgrims from the directives of the merchant adventurers.

In 1627, the Pilgrims divided the land into farm lots and parceled them to each family, particularly along the shores of Plymouth, Kingston, Duxbury, and Marshfield. Mile Standish received 120 acres in Duxbury, where he settled.

Bradford described individual capitalism:

> I answer, seeing that all men have this failing in them, that God in His wisdom saw that another plan of life was fitter for them ...

> So they began to consider how to raise more corn, and obtain a better crop than they had done, so that they might not continue to endure the misery of want ...

> At length after much debate, the Governor, with the advice of the chief among them, allowed each man to plant corn for his own household ...

So every family was assigned a parcel of land, according to the proportion of their number ...

This was very successful. It made all hands very industrious, so that much more corn was planted than otherwise would have been by any means the Governor or any other could devise, and saved him a great deal of trouble, and gave far better satisfaction.

The women now went willing into the field, and took their little ones with them to plant corn, while before they would allege weakness and inability, and to have compelled them would have been thought great tyranny and oppression.

Rush Limbaugh wrote in *See, I Told You So* (New York, NY: Pocket Books, Simon & Schuster Inc., 1993):

When the Pilgrims landed in New England in November, they found, according to Bradford's detailed journal, a cold, barren, desolate wilderness ... The sacrifice they made for freedom was just beginning.

During the first winter, half the Pilgrims-including Bradford's wife-died of either starvation, sickness, or exposure.

When spring finally came, Indians taught the settlers how to plant corn, fish for cod, and skin beavers for coats ...

Thanksgiving is actually explained in some textbooks as a holiday for which the Pilgrims gave thanks to the Indians for saving their lives, rather than as a devout expression of gratitude grounded in the tradition of both the Old and New Testaments ...

The original contract the Pilgrims had entered into with their merchant-sponsors in London called for everything they produced to go into a common store, and each member of the community was entitled to one common share.

All of the land they cleared and the houses they built belonged to the community as well.

Bradford, who had become the new governor of the colony, recognized that this form of collectivism was as costly and destructive to the Pilgrims as that first harsh winter, which had taken so many lives.

He decided to take bold action. Bradford assigned a plot of land to each family to work and manage, thus turning loose the power of the marketplace ...

"This had very good success," wrote Bradford, "for it made all hands industrious, so as much more corn was planted than otherwise would have been" ... Is it possible that supply-side economics could have existed before the 1980's? ...

In no time, the Pilgrims found they had more food than they could eat themselves. So they set up trading posts and exchanged goods with the Indians.

The profits allowed them to pay off their debts to the merchants in London.

And the success and prosperity of the Plymouth settlement attracted more Europeans and began what came to be known as the "Great Puritan Migration."

Limbaugh concluded:

Our history books purposely conceal the fact that these notions were developed by communities of devout Christians who studied the Bible and found it prescribes limited, representative government and free enterprise as the best political and economic systems.

78. PILGRIMS & CHRISTMAS?

In England, during Henry VIII's reign, Christmas celebrations devolved into a sort of Mardi Gras with partying and carousing. Puritans and Pilgrim separatists did not participate in special days, as they considered each day as belonging to the Lord with the only special day being the Sabbath.

When Pilgrims first disembarked the *Mayflower*, the ship master, Christopher Jones, wrote in his ship's log, December 25, 1620:

> At anchor in Plymouth harbor, Christmas Day, but not observed by these colonists, they being opposed to all saints' days, etc ...

> A large party went ashore this morning to fell timber and begin building. They began to erect the first house about twenty feet square for their common use, to receive them and their goods.

A year later, at the end of 1621, William Bradford recorded in *Of Plymouth Plantation*:

> Herewith I shall end this year – except to recall one more incident, rather amusing than serious.

> On Christmas Day the Governor called the people out to work as usual; but most of the new company excused themselves, and said it went against their consciences to work on that day.

> So the Governor told them, if they made it a matter of conscience, he would spare them till they were better informed.

> So he went with the rest, and left them; but on returning from work at noon he found them at play in the street, some pitching the bar, some at stool-ball, and such like sports.

> So he went to them and took away their games,

and told them that it was against his conscience that they should play and others work.

If they made the keeping of the day a matter of devotion, let them remain in their houses; but there should be no gaming and reveling in the streets.

∽

79. DISSENTERS PERSECUTED IN ENGLAND

Back in England, Anglican Archbishop William Laud persecuted Puritans and separatists, sending spies into churches. If pastors departed from the uniformity ordinances, they were arrested.

Prosecution of political enemies was made in the secret "Star Chamber." No lawyers or witnesses were allowed in these arbitrary and oppressive inquisitions.

Though started with the intention of cutting through bureaucratic red tape, Britain's Court of Star Chamber usurped power and became a political weapon for auditing, intimidating, and punishing opponents to the King's uniformity policies.

Individuals were subject to hostile questioning, and if they gave unsatisfactory answers, they were charged with perjury. If they did not answer for fear of self-incrimination, they were held in contempt of court. Abuses of England's Star Chamber led America's founders to include the Fifth Amendment in the U.S. Constitution.

Notoriously biased in favor of the King, the Star Chamber was used in 1637 by William Laud to punish religious dissenter William Prynne who objected to the State's control over religious matters.

Prynne was tied to a pillory – a public pillar– where he had his ears cut off and was branded on the cheeks with the letters "SL" for seditious libel, which Prynne called the "Sign of Laud."

William Laud approved of the Star Chamber's sentence of dissenting Pastor Henry Burton for his "seditious" sermons, resulting in his ears cut off and imprisonment.

When John Bastwick published religious opinions opposing government ordinances, he was brought before the Star Chamber and had his ears cut off then thrown in prison.

Dr. Marshall Foster of the Mayflower Institute (now World History Institute), co-produced with Kirk Cameron the 2012 film *Monumental: In Search of America's National Treasure.*

Dr. Foster described the persecutions of Puritans and Pilgrims in his article "A Shining City on a Hill" (February 27, 2013):

> Four hundred years ago the conflict between tyranny and liberty was red hot ...
>
> When King James died in 1625, his son Charles I ascended to the throne with the arrogance of a Roman emperor. He was the quintessential "divine right" monarch. He declared martial law and suspended the rights of the individual ...
>
> The king's inquisitors at his "Star Chamber" in the tower of London used torture techniques to 'discover the taxpayer's assets ...
>
> A turning point in public opinion took place on January 30, 1637. Three prisoners were locked down in the pillory in London before a huge crowd ...
>
> These men included a Puritan minister, a Christian writer and Dr. John Bastwick, a physician.
>
> What was their crime? They had written pamphlets disagreeing with the king's religious views. The sheriff began by branding the men

with red hot irons on the forehead with an SL for seditious libel.

The Star Chamber forced similar fates on religious dissenter Alexander Leighton, and John Lilburn, who had coined the term "freeborn rights," a term often cited by Supreme Court Justice Hugo Black.

American biographer Edgar Lee Masters (1868–1950) wrote:

> In the Star Chamber the council could inflict any punishment short of death, and frequently sentenced objects of its wrath to the pillory, to whipping and to the cutting off of ears ...

> With each embarrassment to arbitrary power the Star Chamber became emboldened to undertake further usurpation ...

> The Star Chamber finally summoned juries before it for verdicts disagreeable to the government, and fined and imprisoned them.

> It spread terrorism among those who were called to do constitutional acts. It imposed ruinous fines.

Dr. Foster concluded his article "A Shining City on a Hill" (February 27, 2013):

> The tyranny of the king ... finally aroused the Christian sensibilities of the people. They would no longer tolerate burnings or mutilations for matters of conscience on religious views ...

> The persecutions drove tens of thousands of liberty loving believers to follow the Pilgrims to New England where they laid the foundation for the world's most biblically based nation.

John Adams wrote in *A Dissertation on the Canon and Feudal Law*, 1765:

> It was this great struggle that peopled

America ... by a sensible people ... the Puritans...

This people had been so vexed and tortured by the powers of those days, for no other crime than their knowledge and their freedom of inquiry ... they at last resolved to fly to the wilderness for refuge ...

After their arrival here, they ... formed their plan, both of ecclesiastical and civil government, in direct opposition to the canon and the feudal systems ...

Tyranny in every form, shape, and appearance was their disdain ...

They saw clearly, that popular powers must be placed as ... a control, a balance, to the powers of the monarch ... or else it would soon become the man of sin, the whore of Babylon, the mystery of iniquity, a great and detestable system of fraud, violence, and usurpation.

Their greatest concern seems to have been to establish a government of the church more consistent with the Scriptures, and a government of the state more agreeable to the dignity of human nature, than any they had seen in Europe ...

To render the popular power in their new government as great and wise ... as human nature and the Christian religion require it should be, they ... had an utter contempt ... of hereditary, indefeasible right ... of passive obedience and non-resistance ...

They thought all such slavish subordinations were ... inconsistent with ... that religious liberty with which Jesus had made them free.

One of those thrown in prison by William Laud during this time was Edward Winslow, one of the Pilgrim settlers.

8o. EDWARD WINSLOW

Edward Winslow was the only Pilgrim to have his portrait painted. Born in England on October 18, 1595, he became a printer by trade. He joined the Pilgrim separatists and fled with them to Holland in 1608 to escape religious persecution.

This occurred during a period known as the Dutch Golden Age, as Holland was, in a sense, a global superpower, being the world's foremost economic maritime nation.

The predominant faith in Holland was Dutch Reformed, but the country led the world in extending religious toleration to other Christian denominations.

Settling in 1609 in Leiden, Holland, Edward Winslow helped Pilgrim separatist leader William Brewster print illegal religious pamphlets which were smuggled back into England. While there, Brewster taught University of Leiden students.

The University also taught classes in Hebrew, as did England's Universities of Cambridge and Oxford, since 1549 and 1575, respectively.

The King James I of England sent spies and police to Holland where they raided and confiscated the printing press used by Winslow and Brewster.

After years of hardship, Edward Winslow, at the age of 25, departed with the Pilgrims to the New World. His wife had died in the first winter of the Plymouth Colony and he remarried widow Susanna White, whose husband had died that same winter.

Winslow kept the Pilgrims' finances and served as the agent for the Plymouth colony, sailing back and forth bringing supplies, including the colony's first cattle.

On one of his trips back to England, Edward Winslow was thrown in jail for 17 weeks because he had performed marriages in the Plymouth colony without having been ordained.

Pilgrims sought a return to the simplicity of the early church. They believed marriage was only between a man and a woman, created by God for the benefit of their natural and spiritual life: procreation of children to increase Christ's flock; and to avoid the sin of adultery.

The Pilgrims used the Geneva Bible, which gave the words of Jesus in the Book of Matthew 19:4–6:

> And he answered and said unto them, Have ye not read, that he which made them at the beginning, made them male and female, And said, For this cause, shall a man leave father and mother, and cleave unto his wife, and they twain, shall be one flesh.

> Wherefore they are no more twain, but one flesh. Let not man therefore put asunder that, which God hath coupled together.

In 1622, Edward Winslow helped save the Plymouth colony by curing Indian Chief Massasoit of an illness, resulting in the Indians and Pilgrims making a peace treaty which lasted over 50 years. If the chief had not recovered, the Indians would have killed Winslow.

Edward Winslow served three times as the Plymouth Colony's Governor.

ᕤ
81. MUSLIM BARBARY PIRATES

Winslow was witness to another incident. The Pilgrims had borrowed money from English adventurers (investors) to finance their voyage. It took 40 years worth of beaver skins and dried fish to repay their debt due to exorbitant interest rates and losses at sea.

One loss happened in 1625, as Governor Bradford wrote of an encounter with Turkish Muslim pirates (*Of Plymouth Plantation*, trans., Harold Paget, 1909,

The adventurers ... sent over two fishing ships ... The pinnace was ordered to load with corfish ... to bring home to England ... and besides she had some 800 lbs. of beaver, as well as other furs, to a good value from the plantation.

The captain seeing so much lading wished to put aboard the bigger ship for greater safety, but Mr. Edward Winslow, their agent in the business, was bound in a bond to send it to London in the small ship ...

The captain of the big ship ... towed the small ship at his stern all the way over ...

Bradford added:

So they went joyfully home together and had such fine weather that he never cast her off till they were well within the England channel, almost in sight of Plymouth ...

But even there she was unhapply taken by a Turkish man-of-war and carried off to Saller (Morocco) where the captain and crew were made slaves ...

Thus all their hopes were dashed and the joyful news they meant to carry home was turned to heavy tidings ...

Bradford ended:

In the big ship Captain Miles Standish ... arrived at a very bad time ... a plague very deadly in London ... The friendly adventurers were so reduced by their losses last year, and now by the ship taken by the Turks ... that all trade was dead.

✽

82. ISLAMIC KIDNAPPING & SLAVERY

Muslim pirates had terrorized Europeans traveling the seas. In 1605, St. Vincent de Paul was sailing from

Marseille, France, when he was captured by Muslim Turks. He was sold into slavery in Tunis, North Africa.

Fortunately, St. Vincent de Paul was able to convert his owner to Christianity in 1607. He escaped to Europe where he started an order to help the poor, found hospitals, and ransom galley slaves from Barbary North Africa.

Between 1606–1609, Muslim pirates from Algiers captured 466 British and Scottish ships.

Giles Milton's *White Gold: The Extraordinary Story of Thomas Pellow and North Africa's One Million European Slaves* (UK: Hodder & Stoughton Ltd, 2004), records how Muslim corsair pirates raided England in 1625, even sailing up the Thames River.

They attacked the coast of Cornwall, captured 60 villagers at Mount's Bay and 80 at Looe.

Muslim pirates took Lundy Island in Bristol Channel and raised the standard of Islam. By the end of 1625, over 1,000 English subjects were sent to the slave markets of Sale, Morocco.

Between July 4–19, 1627, Algerian and Ottoman Muslim pirates, led by Murat Reis the Younger, raided Iceland, carrying into slavery an estimated 400 from the cities of Reykjavik, Austurland and Vestmannaeyjar.

One captured girl, who had been made a slave concubine in Algeria, was rescued back by King Christian IV of Denmark.

On June 20, 1631, the entire village of Baltimore, Ireland was captured by Muslim pirates, led by Murat Reis the Younger. Only two ever returned. Thomas Osborne Davis wrote in his poem, "The Sack of Baltimore" (1895):

The yell of 'Allah!' breaks above the shriek and roar;

O'blessed God! the Algerine is lord of Baltimore.

Des Ekin wrote in *The Stolen Village: Baltimore and the Barbary Pirates* (O'Brien Press, 2006):

> Here was not a single Christian who was not weeping and who was not full of sadness at the sight of so many honest maidens and so many good women abandoned to the brutality of these barbarians.

Robert C. Davis' book, *Christian Slaves, Muslim Masters: White Slavery in the Mediterranean, the Barbary Coast and Italy 1500–1800* (Palgrave Macmillian, 2003), gives the account of Englishman Francis Knight who was kidnapped and taken to Algiers, where he was made a galley slave for seven years:

> January the 16 day, in the year before nominated 1631; I arrived in Algiers, that City fatal to all Christians, and the butchery of mankind ... my condolation is for the loss of many Christians, taken from their parents and countries, of all sorts and sexes.
>
> Some in Infancy, both by Land and by Sea, being forced to abuses (most incorrigible flagitions) not only so, but bereft of Christian Religion, and means of grace and repentance.
>
> How many thousands of the Nazarian nations have been and are continually lost by that monster, what rational creature can be ignorant of?

❧

83. WINSLOW & ADMIRAL PENN

Edward Winslow sailed back to England after the English Civil War, where he published pamphlets defending the New England colonies: *Hypocrisy Unmasked* (1646); *New England's Salamander Discovered* (1647); *Introduction to Glorious Progress of the Gospel Amongst the Indians in New England* (1649).

Winslow served in briefly in Oliver Cromwell's Puritan army during England's Civil War, 1642–1651.

He sailed with Admiral Sir William Penn, father of Pennsylvania's founder, in an unsuccessful attempt to capture Santo Domingo, Hispaniola, from Spain.

Admiral Penn then sailed to the Island of Jamaica and captured it in 1655. On the way, Edward Winslow contracted the deadly disease of yellow fever and died.

✑

84. ONE CANDLE MAY LIGHT A THOUSAND

Governor Bradford wrote in *Of Plymouth Plantation*:

> They shook off the yoke of anti-christian bondage, and as ye Lord's free people, joined themselves (by a covenant of the Lord) into a church estate, in ye fellowship of ye Gospel, to walk in all his ways ... whatsoever it should cost them, the Lord assisting them ...
>
> All great and honorable actions are accompanied with great difficulties, and must be enterprised and overcome with answerable courages.
>
> It was granted that the dangers were great, but not desperate, and the difficulties were many but not invincible ...and all of them, through the help of God, by fortitude and patience, might either be borne or overcome ...

Bradford added:

> Their ends were good and honorable, their calling lawful and urgent, and therefore they might expect the blessing of God in their proceeding; yea, though they should lose their lives in this action ...
>
> Thus out of small beginnings greater things have been produced by His hand that made all things of nothing ...

and, as one small candle may light a
thousand, so the light here kindled hath shone
unto many, yea in some sort to our whole
nation; let the glorious name of Jehovah have
all the praise.

෴

85. DANIEL WEBSTER AT PLYMOUTH ROCK

At the Bicentennial Celebration of the landing of the
Pilgrims at Plymouth Rock, Secretary of State Daniel
Webster stated December 22, 1820:

Let us be thankful that we have lived to
see ... the third century of the history of New
England ... to the commemoration of the
landing of the Pilgrims ...

The day which saw them, weary and
distressed, broken in every thing but spirit,
poor in all but faith and courage, at last
secure from the dangers of wintry seas, and
impressing this shore with the first footsteps
of civilized man ...

Standing in this relation to our ancestors
and our posterity, we are assembled on this
memorable spot ...

We have come to this Rock, to record here
our homage for our Pilgrim Fathers ... our
attachment to those principles of civil and
religious liberty, which they encountered the
dangers of the ocean, the storms of heaven, the
violence of savages, disease, exile, and famine,
to enjoy and to establish ...

Webster continued:

There is a ... sort of genius of the place,
which ... awes us. We feel that we are on the
spot where the first scene of our history was
laid; where the hearths and altars of New
England were first placed; where Christianity,
and civilization ... made their first lodgement,

in a vast extent of country ...

We are here, at the season of the year at which the event took place ... We cast our eyes abroad on the ocean, and we see where the little bark, with the interesting group upon its deck, made its slow progress to the shore.

We look around us, and behold the hills and promontories where the anxious eyes of our fathers first saw the places of habitation and of rest. We feel the cold which benumbed, and listen to the winds which pierced them. Beneath us is the Rock, on which New England received the feet of the Pilgrims.

We seem even to behold them, as they struggle with the elements, and, with toilsome efforts, gain the shore.

We listen to the chiefs in council; we see the unexampled exhibition of female fortitude and resignation; we hear the whisperings of youthful impatience, and we see ... chilled and shivering childhood, houseless, but for a mother's arms, couchless, but for a mother's breast, till our own blood almost freezes.

The mild dignity of Carver and of Bradford; the decisive and soldier-like air and manner of Standish; the devout Brewster ... their trust in Heaven; their high religious faith ... all of these seem to belong to this place ...

The settlement of New England by the colony which landed here on the 22nd of December, 1620, although not the first European establishment in what now constitutes the United States, was yet so peculiar in its causes and character ... as to give it a high claim to lasting commemoration ...

"If God prosper us," might have been the ... language of our fathers, when they landed upon this Rock, "... we shall here begin a work which shall last for ages ... We shall fill this ... great continent ... with civilization and Christianity."

Webster continued:

The morning that beamed ... saw the Pilgrims already at home ... a government and a country were to commence, with the very first foundations laid under the divine light of the Christian religion ...

Our ancestors established their system of government on morality and religious sentiment ...

Whatever makes men good Christians, makes them good citizens. Our fathers came here to enjoy their religion free and unmolested ...

Whoever shall hereafter write this part of our history ... will be able to record no ... lawless and despotic acts, or any successful usurpation. His page will contain no exhibition of ... civil authority habitually trampled down by military power, or of a community crushed by the burden of taxation ...

He will speak ... of that happy condition, in which the restraint and coercion of government are almost invisible and imperceptible ...

Webster concluded:

Finally, let us not forget the religious character of our origin. Our fathers were brought hither by their high veneration for the Christian religion. They journeyed by its light, and labored in its hope.

They sought to incorporate its principles with the elements of their society, and to diffuse its influence through all their institutions, civil, political, or literary.

Let us cherish these sentiments ... that that is the happiest society which partakes in the highest degree of the mild and peaceful spirit of Christianity.

◆

86. THEY KNEW THEY WERE PILGRIMS

On September 18, 1982, in a Radio Address to the Nation of Prayer, President Ronald Reagan stated:

> The Plymouth settlers triumphed over hunger, disease, and a cruel Northern wilderness because, in the words of William Bradford, "They knew they were Pilgrims, so they committed themselves to the will of God and resolved to proceed."

Poet Katherine Lee Bates (1859-1929) after seeing the view from Pike's Peak in Colorado, 1892, penned "America the Beautiful," which, in 1920, almost became the U.S. National Anthem. The second verse is:

> O Beautiful for Pilgrims Feet,
> Whose Stern Impassioned Stress
> A Thoroughfare for Freedom Beat
> Across the Wilderness!
> America! America!
> God Mend Thy Every Flaw,
> Confirm Thy Soul in Self-Control
> Thy Liberty in Law!

Samuel Francis Smith (1808-1895) wrote in 1832:

> My Country 'tis of thee,
> Sweet land of liberty,
> Of thee I sing;
> Land where my fathers died,
> Land of the Pilgrim's pride,
> From every mountainside,
> Let freedom ring.

Rev. Martin Luther King, Jr., stated at the Civil Rights March in Washington, D.C., August 28, 1963:

I still have a dream ... deeply rooted in the American dream ... that one day on the red hills of Georgia the sons of former slaves and the sons of former slave owners will be able to sit down together at the table of brotherhood ...

This will be the day when all of God's children will be able to sing with new meaning,

"My country 'tis of thee, sweet land of liberty, of thee I sing. Land where my fathers died, land of the Pilgrims' pride, from every mountainside, let freedom ring."

Woodrow Wilson stated August 4, 1920, at the 300th anniversary of the Pilgrims' Landing at Plymouth:

The influences which the ideals and principles of the Pilgrims with respect to civil liberty and human rights have had upon the formation and growth of our institutions and upon our development and progress as a nation merit ... make fitting a nationwide observance ...

I recommend that the day be fittingly observed in the universities, colleges and schools of our country, to the end that salutary and patriotic lessons may be drawn from the fortitude and perseverance and the ideals of this little band of church-men and women who established on this continent the first self-determined government based on the great principle of just law and its equal application to all, and thus planted the seeds from which has sprung the mighty nation.

Henry Adams (1838-1918), great-grandson of John Adams, wrote in *History of the United States,* 1889-91:

The Pilgrims of Plymouth, the Puritans of Boston, the Quakers of Pennsylvania, all avowed a moral purpose, and began by making institutions that consciously reflected a moral idea.

Dwight Eisenhower addressed the American Legion's Back-to-God, February 7, 1954:

> Out of faith in God, and through faith in themselves as His children, our forefathers designed and built this Republic.
>
> We remember from school days that, aboard a tiny ship of destiny called the *Mayflower*, self-government on our continent was first conceived by the Pilgrim Fathers.
>
> Their immortal compact began with the words, "In the name of God, Amen" ...
>
> In the three centuries that separate the Pilgrims of the *Mayflower* from the chaplains of the *Dorchester*, America's freedom, her courage, her strength, and her progress have had their foundation in faith.

Senate Chaplain Peter Marshall opened the 80th Congress, July 3, 1947:

> Let us, as a nation, be not afraid of standing alone for the rights of men, since we were born that way, as the only nation on earth that came into being "for the glory of God and the advancement of the Christian faith."
>
> We know that we shall be true to the Pilgrim dream when we are true to the God they worshiped.

✑

87. FREEDOM TO WORSHIP GOD

Franklin Roosevelt stated in a Radio Address at Hyde Park, New York, November 6, 1944:

> We people of America have ever had a deep well of religious strength, far back to the days of the Pilgrim Fathers.

Ronald Reagan spoke of the Pilgrims in his National

Day of Prayer Proclamation, March 19, 1981:

> The earliest settlers of this land came in search of religious freedom.

> Landing on a desolate shoreline, they established a spiritual foundation that has served us ever since.

> It was the hard work of our people, the freedom they enjoyed and their faith in God that built this country and made it the envy of the world.

John F. Kennedy stated at the 9th Annual Presidential Prayer Breakfast, at Mayflower Hotel, February 9, 1961:

> This country was founded by men and women who were dedicated ... to two propositions:

> FIRST, a strong religious conviction, and SECONDLY, a recognition that this conviction could flourish only under a system of freedom...

> The Puritans and the Pilgrims of my own section of New England, the Quakers of Pennsylvania, the Catholics of Maryland, the Presbyterians of North Carolina, the Methodists and Baptists who came later, all shared these two great traditions which, like silver threads, have run through the warp and the woof of American history.

Horace Mann wrote in his Twelfth Annual Report to the Massachusetts Board of Education, 1848:

> It was in consequence of laws that invaded the exclusive jurisdiction which our Father in Heaven exercises over his children upon earth, that the Pilgrims fled from their native land to that which is the land of our nativity.

> They sought a residence so remote and so inaccessible, in hopes that the prerogatives of the Divine Magistrate might no longer be set

at naught by the usurpations of the civil power.

Was it not an irreligious and an impious act on the part of the British government to pursue our ancestors with such cruel penalties and privations as to drive them into banishment?

Was it not a religious and pious act in the Pilgrim Fathers to seek a place of refuge where the arm of earthly power could neither restrain them from worshiping God in the manner believed to be most acceptable to him, nor command their worship in a manner believed to be unacceptable?

Poet Felicia Dorothea Browne Hemans (1793-1835) wrote in *The Landing of the Pilgrim Fathers*:

What sought they thus afar?

Bright jewels of the mine?

The wealth of seas, the spoils of war?

They sought a faith's pure shrine!

Ay, call it holy ground,

The soil where they first trod!

They have left unstained what there they found -

Freedom to worship God.

✖

88. MANKIND'S SECOND CHANCE

John Adams wrote in his notes of *A Dissertation on the Canon and Feudal Law,* February 1765:

I always consider the settlement of America with reverence and wonder, as the opening of a grand scene and design in Providence for the illumination of the ignorant, and the emancipation of the slavish part of mankind all over the earth.

Governor William Bradford wrote of the Pilgrims:

Last and not least, they cherished a great hope

and inward zeal of laying good foundations ... for the propagation and advance of the gospel of the kingdom of Christ in the remote parts of the world.

Franklin D. Roosevelt stated October 28, 1936, regarding America's founding:

> Rulers ... increased their power over the common men. The seamen they sent to find gold found instead the way of escape for the common man from those rulers ...
>
> What they found over the Western horizon was not the silk and jewels of Cathay but MANKIND'S SECOND CHANCE – a chance to create a new world after he had almost spoiled an old one ...
>
> The Almighty seems purposefully to have withheld that SECOND CHANCE until the time when men would most need and appreciate liberty ...
>
> Those who came ... had courage ... to abandon language and relatives ... to start ... without influence, without money ...
>
> Perhaps Providence did prepare this American continent to be a place of the SECOND CHANCE.

Poet Ralph Waldo Emerson wrote (*The Atlantic Magazine*, April 1862):

> America is another word for opportunity. Our whole history appears like a last effort of the Divine Providence in behalf of the human race.